LIGHT FOR MY PATH FOR THE WORKPLACE

LIGHT FOR MY PATH
FOR THE
WORKPLACE

Illuminating Selections
from the Bible

HUMBLECREEK
INSPIRATION FOR LIFE

Compiled by Sam Wellman, Jennifer Hahn, and Connie Troyer.

© 2005 by Barbour Publishing, Inc.

ISBN 1-59310-737-4

All Scripture quotations are taken from the King James Version of the Bible.

Cover image © Thinkstock

Published by Humble Creek, P.O. Box 719, Uhrichsville, Ohio 44683

Printed in the United States of America.
5 4 3 2 1

INTRODUCTION

Our world sends many conflicting signals on the important issues of life. How should we approach anger? Why speak with honesty? Is prayer for real? What is true wisdom? So much of our time is put into working, that many of our most challenging faith moments come on the job, when we must choose between what we know is right and what the world expects. However, Christians *can* be successful in their faith and work. The work world is part of God's world, and He can rule over it—if we allow Him to. Whatever our needs, we can find in scripture the principles we need to address the issues we face.

God has answered those questions—and many more—in the pages of His Word, the Bible. This topically-arranged collection of Bible verses is a handy reference to some of the key issues that all people face on the job. In these pages, you'll find carefully selected verses that address topics like adversity, courage, forgiveness, gossip, obedience, pride, and temptation. We hope it will be an encouragement to you as you read, on the job or off.

CONTENTS

ADVERSITY

*Extraordinary afflictions are not always
the punishment of extraordinary sins,
but sometimes the trial of extraordinary graces.*

MATTHEW HENRY

That the trial of your faith, being much more precious than of gold that perisheth, though it be tried with fire, might be found unto praise and honour and glory at the appearing of Jesus Christ.

1 PETER 1:7

The righteous cry, and the LORD heareth, and delivereth them out of all their troubles. Many are the afflictions of the righteous: but the LORD delivereth him out of them all.

PSALM 34:17, 19

But the God of all grace, who hath called us unto his eternal glory by Christ Jesus, after that ye have suffered a while, make you perfect, stablish, strengthen, settle you.

1 PETER 5:10

Blessed are ye, when men shall hate you, and when they shall separate you from their company, and shall reproach you, and cast out your name as evil, for the Son of man's sake.   LUKE 6:22

Though he fall, he shall not be utterly cast down: for the LORD upholdeth him with his hand.   PSALM 37:24

No man ought to lay a cross upon himself,

or to adopt tribulation, as is done in popedom;

but if a cross or tribulation come upon him,

then let him suffer it patiently,

and know that it is good and profitable for him.

MARTIN LUTHER

For this is thankworthy, if a man for conscience toward God endure grief, suffering wrongfully. . . . For even hereunto were ye called: because Christ also suffered for us, leaving us an example, that ye should follow his steps: Who did no sin, neither was guile found in his mouth: Who, when he was reviled, reviled not again; when he suffered, he threatened not; but committed himself to him that judgeth righteously.   1 PETER 2:19, 21–23

For I reckon that the sufferings of this present time are not worthy to be compared with the glory which shall be revealed in us.   ROMANS 8:18

But the salvation of the righteous is of the LORD: he is their strength in the time of trouble.   PSALM 37:39

Is any among you afflicted? let him pray.   JAMES 5:13

For as the sufferings of Christ abound in us, so our consolation also aboundeth by Christ. And whether we be afflicted, it is for your consolation and salvation, which is effectual in the enduring of the same sufferings which we also suffer: or whether we be comforted, it is for your consolation and salvation.

2 CORINTHIANS 1:5–6

If ye be reproached for the name of Christ, happy are ye; for the spirit of glory and of God resteth upon you: on their part he is evil spoken of, but on your part he is glorified.   1 PETER 4:14

These things I have spoken unto you, that in me ye might have peace. In the world ye shall have tribulation: but be of good cheer; I have overcome the world.   JOHN 16:33

But rejoice, inasmuch as ye are partakers of Christ's sufferings; that, when his glory shall be revealed, ye may be glad also with ex-ceeding joy.   1 PETER 4:13

For our light affliction, which is but for a moment, worketh for us a far more exceeding and eternal weight of glory.

2 CORINTHIANS 4:17

The LORD openeth the eyes of the blind: the LORD raiseth them that are bowed down: the LORD loveth the righteous.   PSALM 146:8

Thou art my hiding place; thou shalt preserve me from trouble; thou shalt compass me about with songs of deliverance.

PSALM 32:7

Thou, which hast shewed me great and sore troubles, shalt quicken me again, and shalt bring me up again from the depths of the earth.

PSALM 71:20

The LORD is good, a strong hold in the day of trouble; and he knoweth them that trust in him.   NAHUM 1:7

Why art thou cast down, O my soul? and why art thou disquieted within me? hope thou in God: for I shall yet praise him, who is the health of my countenance, and my God.   PSALM 42:11

Go to the scriptures. . . .

The joyful promises it contains

will be a balsam to all your troubles.

ANDREW JACKSON

My flesh and my heart faileth: but God is the strength of my heart, and my portion for ever.   PSALM 73:26

Yet man is born unto trouble, as the sparks fly upward. I would seek unto God, and unto God would I commit my cause.
                                                      JOB 5:7–8

There shall no evil befall thee, neither shall any plague come nigh thy dwelling. For he shall give his angels charge over thee, to keep thee in all thy ways.   PSALM 91:10–11

They that sow in tears shall reap in joy. He that goeth forth and weepeth, bearing precious seed, shall doubtless come again with rejoicing, bringing his sheaves with him.   PSALM 126:5–6

Behold, God will not cast away a perfect man, neither will he help the evildoers: Till he fill thy mouth with laughing, and thy lips with rejoicing.   JOB 8:20–21

O love the LORD, all ye his saints: for the LORD preserveth the faithful, and plentifully rewardeth the proud doer.   PSALM 31:23

For he hath not despised nor abhorred the affliction of the afflicted; neither hath he hid his face from him; but when he cried unto him, he heard.   PSALM 22:24

The LORD also will be a refuge for the oppressed, a refuge in times of trouble.   PSALM 9:9

Though I walk in the midst of trouble, thou wilt revive me: thou shalt stretch forth thine hand against the wrath of mine enemies, and thy right hand shall save me.   PSALM 138:7

For the LORD will not cast off for ever: But though he cause grief, yet will he have compassion according to the multitude of his mercies. For he doth not afflict willingly nor grieve the children of men.   LAMENTATIONS 3:31–33

If we had no winter,

the spring would not be so pleasant:

If we did not sometimes taste of adversity,

prosperity would not be so welcome.

ANNE BRADSTREET

The LORD is my rock, and my fortress, and my deliverer; my God, my strength, in whom I will trust; my buckler, and the horn of my salvation, and my high tower.   PSALM 18:2

Rejoice not against me, O mine enemy: when I fall, I shall arise; when I sit in darkness, the LORD shall be a light unto me. I will bear the indignation of the LORD, because I have sinned against him, until he plead my cause, and execute judgment for me: he will bring me forth to the light, and I shall behold his righteousness.

MICAH 7:8–9

These things I have spoken unto you, that in me ye might have peace. In the world ye shall have tribulation: but be of good cheer; I have overcome the world.   JOHN 16:33

ANGER

*He best keeps from
anger who remembers
that God is
always looking upon him.*

PLATO

He that is slow to wrath is of great understanding: but he that is hasty of spirit exalteth folly.   PROVERBS 14:29

The LORD is gracious, and full of compassion; slow to anger, and of great mercy.   PSALM 145:8

He that is slow to anger is better than the mighty; and he that ruleth his spirit than he that taketh a city.   PROVERBS 16:32

Cease from anger, and forsake wrath: fret not thyself in any wise to do evil.   PSALM 37:8

He that is soon angry dealeth foolishly.   PROVERBS 14:17

Wherefore, my beloved brethren, let every man be swift to hear, slow to speak, slow to wrath: for the wrath of man worketh not the righteousness of God.   JAMES 1:19–20

But now ye also put off all these; anger, wrath, malice, blasphemy, filthy communication out of your mouth.   COLOSSIANS 3:8

When angry, count ten before you speak;

if very angry, one hundred.

HORACE

A soft answer turneth away wrath: but grievous words stir up anger.   PROVERBS 15:1

Do all things without murmurings and disputings.   PHILIPPIANS 2:14

Be not hasty in thy spirit to be angry: for anger resteth in the bosom of fools.   ECCLESIASTES 7:9

Be ye angry, and sin not: let not the sun go down upon your wrath.   EPHESIANS 4:26

Fathers, provoke not your children to anger, lest they be discouraged.   COLOSSIANS 3:21

It is better to dwell in the wilderness, than with a contentious and an angry woman.   PROVERBS 21:19

Make no friendship with an angry man; and with a furious man thou shalt not go: Lest thou learn his ways, and get a snare to thy soul. PROVERBS 22:24–25

Let all bitterness, and wrath, and anger, and clamour, and evil speaking, be put away from you, with all malice: And be ye kind one to another, tenderhearted, forgiving one another, even as God for Christ's sake hath forgiven you. EPHESIÀNS 4:31–32

A wrathful man stirreth up strife: but he that is slow to anger appeaseth strife. PROVERBS 15:18

An angry man stirreth up strife, and a furious man aboundeth in transgression. PROVERBS 29:22

The discretion of a man deferreth his anger; and it is his glory to pass over a transgression. PROVERBS 19:11

But I say unto you, that whosoever is angry with his brother without a cause shall be in danger of the judgment: and whosoever shall say to his brother, Raca, shall be in danger of the council: but whosoever shall say, Thou fool, shall be in danger of hell fire. MATTHEW 5:22

Better is a dry morsel, and quietness therewith, than an house full of sacrifices with strife. PROVERBS 17:1

Dearly beloved, avenge not yourselves, but rather give place unto wrath: for it is written, Vengeance is mine; I will repay, saith the Lord. Therefore if thine enemy hunger, feed him; if he thirst, give him drink: for in so doing thou shalt heap coals of fire on his head. Be not overcome of evil, but overcome evil with good. ROMANS 12:19–21

Weeping may endure for a night, but joy cometh in the morning. PSALM 30:5

When anger enters the mind,

wisdom departs.

THOMAS À KEMPIS

If thine enemy be hungry, give him bread to eat; and if he be thirsty, give him water to drink: For thou shalt heap coals of fire upon his head, and the LORD shall reward thee.

PROVERBS 25:21–22

CHARITY

The desire of power in excess caused the angels to fall;
the desire of knowledge in excess caused man to fall;
but in charity there is no excess,
neither can angel or man come in danger by it.

FRANCIS BACON

Blessed is he that considereth the poor: the LORD will deliver him in time of trouble. The LORD will preserve him, and keep him alive; and he shall be blessed upon the earth: and thou wilt not deliver him unto the will of his enemies.   PSALM 41:1–2

He that hath pity upon the poor lendeth unto the LORD; and that which he hath given will he pay him again.   PROVERBS 19:17

Sell that ye have, and give alms; provide yourselves bags which wax not old, a treasure in the heavens that faileth not, where no thief approacheth, neither moth corrupteth.   LUKE 12:33

But when thou makest a feast, call the poor, the maimed, the lame, the blind: And thou shalt be blessed; for they cannot recompense thee: for thou shalt be recompensed at the resurrection of the just.

LUKE 14:13–14

He that despiseth his neighbour sinneth: but he that hath mercy on the poor, happy is he.   PROVERBS 14:21

Give, and it shall be given unto you; good measure, pressed down, and shaken together, and running over, shall men give into your bosom. For with the same measure that ye mete withal it shall be measured to you again.   LUKE 6:38

Charity should begin at home but should not stay there.

PHILLIPS BROOKS

He hath dispersed, he hath given to the poor; his righteousness endureth for ever; his horn shall be exalted with honour.

PSALM 112:9

And now abideth faith, hope, charity, these three; but the greatest of these is charity.   1 CORINTHIANS 13:13

He that giveth unto the poor shall not lack: but he that hideth his eyes shall have many a curse.   PROVERBS 28:27

Every man according as he purposeth in his heart, so let him give; not grudgingly, or of necessity: for God loveth a cheerful giver.

2 CORINTHIANS 9:7

I have been young, and now am old; yet have I not seen the righteous forsaken, nor his seed begging bread.   PSALM 37:25

There is that scattereth, and yet increaseth; and there is that withholdeth more than is meet, but it tendeth to poverty. The liberal soul shall be made fat: and he that watereth shall be watered also himself.

PROVERBS 11:24–25

Charge them that are rich in this world, that they be not high-minded, nor trust in uncertain riches, but in the living God, who giveth us richly all things to enjoy; that they do good, that they be rich in good works, ready to distribute, willing to communicate.

1 TIMOTHY 6:17–18

Cast thy bread upon the waters: for thou shalt find it after many days.

ECCLESIASTES 11:1

And if thou draw out thy soul to the hungry, and satisfy the afflicted soul; then shall thy light rise in obscurity, and thy darkness be as the noon day.

ISAIAH 58:10

It is not to deal thy bread to the hungry, and that thou bring the poor that are cast out to thy house? when thou seest the naked, that thou cover him; and that thou hide not thyself from thine own flesh? Then shall thy light break forth as the morning, and thine health shall spring forth speedily: and thy righteousness shall go before thee; the glory of the LORD shall be thy reward.

ISAIAH 58:7–8

And the Levite, (because he hath no part nor inheritance with thee,) and the stranger, and the fatherless, and the widow, which are within thy gates, shall come, and shall eat and be satisfied; that the LORD thy God may bless thee in all the work of thine hand which thou doest.

DEUTERONOMY 14:29

Then Jesus beholding him loved him, and said unto him, One thing thou lackest: go thy way, sell whatsoever thou hast, and give to the poor, and thou shalt have treasure in heaven: and come, take up the cross, and follow me.

MARK 10:21

He is ever merciful, and lendeth; and his seed is blessed.

PSALM 37:26

Take heed that ye do not your alms before men, to be seen of them: otherwise ye have no reward of your Father which is in heaven. Therefore when thou doest thine alms, do not sound a trumpet before thee, as the hypocrites do in the synagogues and in the streets, that they may have glory of men. Verily I say unto you, They have their reward. But when thou doest alms, let not thy left hand know what thy right hand doeth: That thine alms may be in secret: and thy Father which seeth in secret himself shall reward thee openly.

MATTHEW 6:1–4

If you haven't got any charity in your heart,

you have the worst kind of heart trouble.

BOB HOPE

Then shall the King say unto them on his right hand, Come, ye blessed of my Father, inherit the kingdom prepared for you from the foundation of the world: For I was an hungred, and ye gave me meat: I was thirsty, and ye gave me drink: I was a stranger, and ye took me in: Naked, and ye clothed me: I was sick, and ye visited me: I was in prison, and ye came unto me. Then shall the righteous answer him, saying, Lord, when saw we thee an hungred, and fed thee? or thirsty, and gave thee drink? When saw we thee a stranger, and took thee in? or naked, and clothed thee? Or when saw we thee sick, or in prison, and came unto thee? And the King shall answer and say unto them, Verily I say unto you, Inasmuch as ye have done it unto one of the least of these my brethren, ye have done it unto me.

MATTHEW 25:34–40

COMFORT

We need never shout
across the spaces to an absent God.
He is nearer than our own soul,
closer than our most secret thoughts.

A. W. TOZER

Come unto me, all ye that labour and are heavy laden, and I will
give you rest. MATTHEW 11:28

And it shall come to pass in the day that the LORD shall give thee
rest from thy sorrow, and from thy fear, and from the hard bondage
wherein thou wast made to serve. ISAIAH 14:3

And God shall wipe away all tears from their eyes; and there shall
be no more death, neither sorrow, nor crying, neither shall there be
any more pain: for the former things are passed away.
REVELATION 21:4

Yea, though I walk through the valley of the shadow of death, I will fear no evil: for thou art with me; thy rod and thy staff they comfort me.   PSALM 23:4

For the Lord himself shall descend from heaven with a shout, with the voice of the archangel, and with the trump of God: and the dead in Christ shall rise first: Then we which are alive and remain shall be caught up together with them in the clouds, to meet the Lord in the air: and so shall we ever be with the Lord. Wherefore comfort one another with these words.   1 THESSALONIANS 4:16–18

O God, our help in ages past,

Our hope for years to come,

Our shelter from the stormy blast,

And our eternal home.

ISAAC WATTS

God is our refuge and strength, a very present help in trouble. Therefore will not we fear, though the earth be removed, and though the mountains be carried into the midst of the sea; though the waters thereof roar and be troubled, though the mountains shake with the swelling thereof.   PSALM 46:1–3

But they that wait upon the LORD shall renew their strength; they shall mount up with wings as eagles; they shall run, and not be weary; and they shall walk, and not faint.   ISAIAH 40:31

And I will pray the Father, and he shall give you another Comforter, that he may abide with you for ever.   JOHN 14:16

Comfort ye, comfort ye my people, saith your God.   ISAIAH 40:1

The Spirit of the Lord GOD is upon me; because the LORD hath anointed me to preach good tidings unto the meek; he hath sent me to bind up the brokenhearted, to proclaim liberty to the captives, and the opening of the prison to them that are bound; to proclaim the acceptable year of the LORD, and the day of vengeance of our God; to comfort all that mourn.   ISAIAH 61:1–2

Yet man is born unto trouble, as the sparks fly upward. I would seek unto God, and unto God would I commit my cause.
                                                                   JOB 5:7–8

Casting all your care upon him; for he careth for you. 1 PETER 5:7

Blessed are they that mourn: for they shall be comforted.
                                                                MATTHEW 5:4

The Lord GOD will wipe away tears from off all faces.
                                                                 ISAIAH 25:8

Weeping may endure for a night, but joy cometh in the morning.
                                                                 PSALM 30:5

Blessed be God, even the Father of our Lord Jesus Christ, the Father of mercies, and the God of all comfort; who comforteth us in all our tribulation, that we may be able to comfort them which are in any trouble, by the comfort wherewith we ourselves are comforted of God. For as the sufferings of Christ abound in us, so our consolation also aboundeth by Christ.   2 CORINTHIANS 1:3–5

And, lo, I am with you alway, even unto the end of the world.
                                                              MATTHEW 28:20

I will not leave you comfortless: I will come to you.   JOHN 14:18

Though I walk in the midst of trouble, thou wilt revive me: thou shalt stretch forth thine hand against the wrath of mine enemies, and thy right hand shall save me.   PSALM 138:7

The LORD is my rock, and my fortress, and my deliverer; my God, my strength, in whom I will trust; my buckler, and the horn of my salvation, and my high tower.   PSALM 18:2

The Christian life is not a constant high.

I have my moments of deep discouragement.

I have to go to God in prayer

with tears in my eyes and say,

"O God, forgive me," or "Help me."

BILLY GRAHAM

For he hath not despised nor abhorred the affliction of the afflicted; neither hath he hid his face from him; but when he cried unto him, he heard.   PSALM 22:24

Though he fall, he shall not be utterly cast down: for the LORD upholdeth him with his hand.   PSALM 37:24

The LORD is good, a strong hold in the day of trouble; and he knoweth them that trust in him.   NAHUM 1:7

These things I have spoken unto you, that in me ye might have peace. In the world ye shall have tribulation: but be of good cheer; I have overcome the world.   JOHN 16:33

But the salvation of the righteous is of the LORD: he is their strength in the time of trouble. PSALM 37:39

Cast thy burden upon the LORD, and he shall sustain thee: he shall never suffer the righteous to be moved. PSALM 55:22

The LORD also will be a refuge for the oppressed, a refuge in times of trouble. PSALM 9:9

For the LORD will not cast off for ever: But though he cause grief, yet will he have compassion according to the multitude of his mercies. For he doth not afflict willingly nor grieve the children of men. LAMENTATIONS 3:31–33

Wait on the LORD: be of good courage, and he shall strengthen thine heart: wait, I say, on the LORD. PSALM 27:14

CONTENTMENT

If the Lord sets you to guard a lonely post
in perfect stillness from all active work,
you ought to be just as content as
to be in the midst of the active warfare.
It is no virtue to love the Master's work
better than the Master's will.

HANNAH WHITALL SMITH

A merry heart doeth good like a medicine: but a broken spirit drieth the bones.   PROVERBS 17:22

All the days of the afflicted are evil: but he that is of a merry heart hath a continual feast.   PROVERBS 15:15

A sound heart is the life of the flesh: but envy the rottenness of the bones.   PROVERBS 14:30

Let your conversation be without covetousness; and be content with such things as ye have: for he hath said, I will never leave thee, nor forsake thee.   HEBREWS 13:5

A man travels the world over

in search of what he needs

and returns home to find it.

GEORGE MOORE

But godliness with contentment is great gain. For we brought nothing into this world, and it is certain we can carry nothing out. And having food and raiment let us be therewith content.

1 TIMOTHY 6:6–8

Let not thine heart envy sinners: but be thou in the fear of the LORD all the day long. For surely there is an end; and thine expectation shall not be cut off.   PROVERBS 23:17–18

The fear of the LORD tendeth to life: and he that hath it shall abide satisfied; he shall not be visited with evil.   PROVERBS 19:23

And the soldiers likewise demanded of him, saying, And what shall we do? And he said unto them, Do violence to no man, neither accuse any falsely; and be content with your wages.

LUKE 3:14

For I have learned, in whatsoever state I am, therewith to be content.

PHILIPPIANS 4:11

CONVERSATION

Speak softly.
It is far better to rule by love than fear.
Speak softly.
Let no harsh words mar the good
we may do here.

ISAAC WATTS

In the multitude of words there wanteth not sin: but he that refraineth his lips is wise.   PROVERBS 10:19

A word fitly spoken is like apples of gold in pictures of silver.
                                                  PROVERBS 25:11

I said, I will take heed to my ways, that I sin not with my tongue: I will keep my mouth with a bridle, while the wicked is before me.
                                                      PSALM 39:1

Only let your conversation be as it becometh the gospel of Christ: that whether I come and see you, or else be absent, I may hear of your affairs, that ye stand fast in one spirit, with one mind striving together for the faith of the gospel; and in nothing terrified by your adversaries: which is to them an evident token of perdition, but to you of salvation, and that of God.   Philippians 1:27–28

For though I would desire to glory, I shall not be a fool; for I will say the truth: but now I forbear, lest any man should think of me above that which he seeth me to be, or that he heareth of me.
                                                                    2 Corinthians 12:6

A fool uttereth all his mind: but a wise man keepeth it in till afterwards.   Proverbs 29:11

But now ye also put off all these; anger, wrath, malice, blasphemy, filthy communication out of your mouth.   Colossians 3:8

A soft answer turneth away wrath: but grievous words stir up anger.   Proverbs 15:1

A talebearer revealeth secrets: but he that is of a faithful spirit concealeth the matter.   Proverbs 11:13

Set a watch, O Lord, before my mouth; keep the door of my lips.
                                                                    Psalm 141:3

There is that speaketh like the piercings of a sword: but the tongue of the wise is health.   Proverbs 12:18

If any man offend not in word, the same is a perfect man, and able also to bridle the whole body.   James 3:2

A time to rend, and a time to sew; a time to keep silence, and a time to speak.   Ecclesiastes 3:7

A man hath joy by the answer of his mouth: and a word spoken in due season, how good is it!   PROVERBS 15:23

The heart of the righteous studieth to answer: but the mouth of the wicked poureth out evil things.   PROVERBS 15:28

A dearth of words a woman need not fear;

But 'tis a task indeed to learn to hear:

In that the skill of conversation lies;

That shows and makes you both polite and wise.

EDWARD YOUNG

Let your speech be alway with grace, seasoned with salt, that ye may know how ye ought to answer every man.   COLOSSIANS 4:6

Let your conversation be without covetousness. . .for he hath said, I will never leave thee, nor forsake thee.   HEBREWS 13:5

COURAGE

Down through the centuries in times of trouble,
temptations, trial, bereavement, and crisis,
God has brought courage to the hearts of
those who love Him.
The Bible is crowded with
assurances of God's help and comfort
in every kind of troublewhich might cause
fears to arise in the human heart.

BILLY GRAHAM

Wait on the LORD: be of good courage, and he shall strengthen thine heart: wait, I say, on the LORD.   PSALM 27:14

And now, little children, abide in him; that, when he shall appear, we may have confidence, and not be ashamed before him at his coming.   1 JOHN 2:28

For God hath not given us the spirit of fear; but of power, and of love, and of a sound mind.   2 TIMOTHY 1:7

Only let your conversation be as it becometh the gospel of Christ: that whether I come and see you, or else be absent, I may hear of your affairs, that ye stand fast in one spirit, with one mind striving together for the faith of the gospel; and in nothing terrified by your adversaries: which is to them an evident token of perdition, but to you of salvation, and that of God.   PHILIPPIANS 1:27–28

The sea is dangerous and its storms terrible,

but these obstacles have never been

sufficient reason to remain ashore. . . .

Unlike the mediocre, intrepid spirits seek victory

over those things that seem impossible. . . .

It is with an iron will that they embark on

the most daring of all endeavors. . .

to meet the shadowy future without fear

and conquer the unknown.

FERDINAND MAGELLAN

But now thus saith the LORD that created thee, O Jacob, and he that formed thee, O Israel, Fear not: for I have redeemed thee, I have called thee by thy name: thou art mine.   Isaiah 43:1

So that we may boldly say, The Lord is my helper, and I will not fear what man shall do unto me.   HEBREWS 13:6

In the fear of the LORD is strong confidence: and his children shall have a place of refuge.   PROVERBS 14:26

Watch ye, stand fast in the faith, quit you like men, be strong.
                                           1 CORINTHIANS 16:13

And thou, son of man, be not afraid of them, neither be afraid of their words, though briers and thorns be with thee, and thou dost dwell among scorpions: be not afraid of their words, nor be dismayed at their looks, though they be a rebellious house.   EZEKIEL 2:6

The wicked flee when no man pursueth: but the righteous are bold as a lion.   PROVERBS 28:1

Having therefore, brethren, boldness to enter into the holiest by the blood of Jesus.   HEBREWS 10:19

Be of good courage, and he shall strengthen your heart, all ye that hope in the LORD.   PSALM 31:24

In whom we have boldness and access with confidence by the faith of him.   EPHESIANS 3:12

For the LORD shall be thy confidence, and shall keep thy foot from being taken.   PROVERBS 3:26

Trust in the LORD, and do good; so shalt thou dwell in the land, and verily thou shalt be fed.   PSALM 37:3

He giveth power to the faint; and to them that have no might he increaseth strength.   ISAIAH 40:29

DEATH/ETERNAL LIFE

Christ is the Son of God.
He died to atone for men's sin,
and after three days rose again.
This is the most important fact in the universe.
I die believing in Christ.

WATCHMAN NEE
From a note found under his pillow in prison at his death.

Yea, though I walk through the valley of the shadow of death, I will fear no evil: for thou art with me; thy rod and thy staff they comfort me. PSALM 23:4

That whosoever believeth in him should not perish, but have eternal life. JOHN 3:15

Much more then, being now justified by his blood, we shall be saved from wrath through him. ROMANS 5:9

Forasmuch then as the children are partakers of flesh and blood, he also himself likewise took part of the same; that through death he might destroy him that had the power of death, that is, the devil; and deliver them who through fear of death were all their lifetime subject to bondage.   HEBREWS 2:14–15

For this God is our God for ever and ever: he will be our guide even unto death.   PSALM 48:14

But God will redeem my soul from the power of the grave: for he shall receive me.   PSALM 49:15

My flesh and my heart faileth: but God is the strength of my heart, and my portion for ever.   PSALM 73:26

He will swallow up death in victory; and the LORD God will wipe away tears from off all faces.   ISAIAH 25:8

Behold, I shew you a mystery; we shall not all sleep, but we shall all be changed, in a moment, in the twinkling of an eye, at the last trump: for the trumpet shall sound, and the dead shall be raised incorruptible, and we shall be changed. For this corruptible must put on incorruption, and this mortal must put on immortality. So when this corruptible shall have put on incorruption, and this mortal shall have put on immortality, then shall be brought to pass the saying that is written, Death is swallowed up in victory.   1 CORINTHIANS 15:51–54

I will ransom them from the power of the grave; I will redeem them from death: O death, I will be thy plagues; O grave, I will be thy destruction: repentance shall be hid from mine eyes.   HOSEA 13:14

Precious in the sight of the LORD is the death of his saints.   PSALM 116:15

Mark the perfect man, and behold the upright: for the end of that man is peace.   PSALM 37:37

But though our outward man perish, yet the inward man is renewed day by day.   2 CORINTHIANS 4:16

Asleep in Jesus! Blessèd sleep,

From which none ever wakes to weep;

A calm and undisturbed repose,

Unbroken by the last of foes.

Asleep in Jesus! Oh, how sweet,

To be for such a slumber meet,

With holy confidence to sing

That death has lost his venomed sting.

MARGARET MACKAY

For I am persuaded, that neither death, nor life, nor angels, nor principalities, nor powers, nor things present, nor things to come, nor height, nor depth, nor any other creature, shall be able to separate us from the love of God, which is in Christ Jesus our Lord.
                                              ROMANS 8:38–39

God. . .will render to every man according to his deeds: To them who by patient continuance in well doing seek for glory and honour and immortality, eternal life.   ROMANS 2:5–7

And I give unto them eternal life; and they shall never perish, neither shall any man pluck them out of my hand.   John 10:28

For the wages of sin is death; but the gift of God is eternal life through Jesus Christ our Lord.   ROMANS 6:23

And this is the record, that God hath given to us eternal life, and this life is in his Son.   1 JOHN 5:11

Jesus said unto her, I am the resurrection, and the life: he that believeth in me, though he were dead, yet shall he live: And whosoever liveth and believeth in me shall never die. Believest thou this?
          JOHN 11:25–26

And when the chief Shepherd shall appear, ye shall receive a crown of glory that fadeth not away.   1 PETER 5:4

Henceforth there is laid up for me a crown of righteousness, which the Lord, the righteous judge, shall give me at that day: and not to me only, but unto all them also that love his appearing.
          2 TIMOTHY 4:8

For we know that if our earthly house of this tabernacle were dissolved, we have a building of God, an house not made with hands, eternal in the heavens.   2 CORINTHIANS 5:1

Verily, verily, I say unto you, He that heareth my word, and believeth on him that sent me, hath everlasting life, and shall not come into condemnation; but is passed from death unto life.
          JOHN 5:24

In my Father's house are many mansions: if it were not so, I would have told you. I go to prepare a place for you. And if I go and prepare a place for you, I will come again, and receive you unto myself; that where I am, there ye may be also.   JOHN 14:2–3

The best we can hope for in this life

is a knothole peek at the shining realities ahead.

Yet a glimpse is enough.

It's enough to convince our hearts

that whatever sufferings and sorrows currently assail us

aren't worthy of comparison to that

which waits over the horizon.

JONI EARECKSON TADA

Search the scriptures; for in them ye think ye have eternal life: and they are they which testify of me.   JOHN 5:39

DEPENDABILITY

Steer clear of anyone who values
cleverness above dependability,
expedience above integrity,
and charm above character.

WILLIAM ARTHUR WARD

And the Lord said, Who then is that faithful and wise steward, whom his lord shall make ruler over his household, to give them their portion of meat in due season?   LUKE 12:42

And he spake a parable unto them to this end, that men ought always to pray, and not to faint.   LUKE 18:1

Be not carried about with divers and strange doctrines. For it is a good thing that the heart be established with grace; not with meats, which have not profited them that have been occupied therein.   HEBREWS 13:9

But he that shall endure unto the end, the same shall be saved.
MATTHEW 24:13

And ye have forgotten the exhortation which speaketh unto you as unto children, My son, despise not thou the chastening of the Lord, nor faint when thou art rebuked of him.   HEBREWS 12:5

Teach me, O LORD, the way of thy statutes; and I shall keep it unto the end.   PSALM 119:33

Ability without dependability has no value.

UNKNOWN

Let a man so account of us, as of the ministers of Christ, and stewards of the mysteries of God. Moreover it is required in stewards, that a man be found faithful.   1 CORINTHIANS 4:1–2

Wherefore we labour, that, whether present or absent, we may be accepted of him.   2 CORINTHIANS 5:9

Let your loins be girded about, and your lights burning; and ye yourselves like unto men that wait for their lord, when he will return from the wedding; that when he cometh and knocketh, they may open unto him immediately.   LUKE 12:35–36

For if any be a hearer of the word, and not a doer, he is like unto a man beholding his natural face in a glass: For he beholdeth himself, and goeth his way, and straightway forgetteth what manner of man he was. But whoso looketh into the perfect law of liberty, and continueth therein, he being not a forgetful hearer, but a doer of the work, this man shall be blessed in his deed.   JAMES 1:23–25

DUTY

The best things are nearest:
breath in your nostrils, light in your eyes,
flowers at your feet, duties at your hand,
the path of Right just before you. . . .
Do life's plain common work as it comes,
certain that daily duties and daily bread
are the sweetest things in life.

ROBERT LOUIS STEVENSON

And he sought God in the days of Zechariah, who had understanding in the visions of God: and as long as he sought the Lord, God made him to prosper. 2 CHRONICLES 26:5

Now therefore, if ye will obey my voice indeed, and keep my covenant, then ye shall be a peculiar treasure unto me above all people: for all the earth is mine. EXODUS 19:5

And why call ye me, Lord, and do not the things which I say?

LUKE 6:46

Thou shalt keep therefore his statutes, and his commandments, which I command thee this day, that it may go well with thee, and with thy children after thee, and that thou mayest prolong thy days upon the earth, which the LORD thy God giveth thee, for ever.

DEUTERONOMY 4:40

Duty is ours; results are God's.

JOHN QUINCY ADAMS

When a man's ways please the LORD, he maketh even his enemies to be at peace with him.   PROVERBS 16:7

Save when there shall be no poor among you; for the LORD shall greatly bless thee in the land which the LORD thy God giveth thee for an inheritance to possess it: Only if thou carefully hearken unto the voice of the LORD thy God, to observe to do all these commandments which I command thee this day.

DEUTERONOMY 15:4–5

See, I have set before thee this day life and good, and death and evil; in that I command thee this day to love the LORD thy God, to walk in his ways, and to keep his commandments and his statutes and his judgments, that thou mayest live and multiply: and the LORD thy God shall bless thee in the land whither thou goest to possess it.   DEUTERONOMY 30:15–16

If ye be willing and obedient, ye shall eat the good of the land.

ISAIAH 1:19

If they obey and serve him, they shall spend their days in prosperity, and their years in pleasures. JOB 36:11

And shewing mercy unto thousands of them that love me, and keep my commandments. EXODUS 20:6

Observe and hear all these words which I command thee, that it may go well with thee, and with thy children after thee for ever, when thou doest that which is good and right in the sight of the LORD thy God. DEUTERONOMY 12:28

And ye shall be hated of all men for my name's sake: but he that endureth to the end shall be saved. MATTHEW 10:22

ENCOURAGEMENT

If I can do some good today,
If I can serve along life's way,
If I can something helpful say,
Lord, show me how.

If I can right a human wrong,
If I can help to make one strong,
If I can cheer with smile or song,
Lord, show me how.

If I can aid one in distress,
If I can make a burden less,
If I can spread more happiness,
Lord, show me how.

GRENVILLE KLEISER

I can do all things through Christ which strengtheneth me.

PHILIPPIANS 4:13

Therefore, brethren, stand fast, and hold the traditions which ye have been taught, whether by word, or our epistle. Now our Lord Jesus Christ himself, and God, even our Father, which hath loved us, and hath given us everlasting consolation and good hope through grace, comfort your hearts, and stablish you in every good word and work.   2 THESSALONIANS 2:15–17

He giveth power to the faint; and to them that have no might he increaseth strength.   ISAIAH 40:29

And when they bring you unto the synagogues, and unto magistrates, and powers, take ye no thought how or what thing ye shall answer, or what ye shall say: For the Holy Ghost shall teach you in the same hour what ye ought to say.   LUKE 12:11–12

All scripture is given by inspiration of God, and is profitable for doctrine, for reproof, for correction, for instruction in righteousness.

2 TIMOTHY 3:16

Wherefore comfort yourselves together, and edify one another, even as also ye do.   1 THESSALONIANS 5:11

Brethren, if any of you do err from the truth, and one convert him; let him know, that he which converteth the sinner from the error of his way shall save a soul from death, and shall hide a multitude of sins.   JAMES 5:19–20

And whether we be afflicted, it is for your consolation and salvation, which is effectual in the enduring of the same sufferings which we also suffer: or whether we be comforted, it is for your consolation and salvation.   2 CORINTHIANS 1:6

If there be therefore any consolation in Christ, if any comfort of love, if any fellowship of the Spirit, if any bowels and mercies, fulfil ye my joy, that ye be likeminded, having the same love, being of one accord, of one mind. Look not every man on his own things, but every man also on the things of others.   PHILIPPIANS 2:1–2, 4

Bear ye one another's burdens, and so fulfil the law of Christ.
GALATIANS 6:2

The world is in dire need

of encouragers.

G. E. DEAN

Ye are witnesses, and God also, how holily and justly and unblameably we behaved ourselves among you that believe: As ye know how we exhorted and comforted and charged every one of you, as a father doth his children, that ye would walk worthy of God, who hath called you unto his kingdom and glory. For this cause also thank we God without ceasing, because, when ye received the word of God which ye heard of us, ye received it not as the word of men, but as it is in truth, the word of God, which effectually worketh also in you that believe.   1 THESSALONIANS 2:10–13

ENEMIES

In the secret of God's tabernacle no enemy can find us,
and no troubles can reach us.
The pride of man and the strife of tongues
find no entrance into the pavilion of God.
The secret of his presence is a more secure refuge
than a thousand Gibraltars.
I do not mean that no trials come.
They may come in abundance,
but they cannot penetrate into the sanctuary of the soul,
and we may dwell in perfect peace
even in the midst of life fiercest storms.

HANNAH WHITALL SMITH

Bless them which persecute you: bless, and curse not.

ROMANS 12:14

When a man's ways please the LORD, he maketh even his enemies to be at peace with him.   PROVERBS 16:7

Therefore if thine enemy hunger, feed him; if he thirst, give him drink: for in so doing thou shalt heap coals of fire on his head. Be not overcome of evil, but overcome evil with good.
                                                    ROMANS 12:20–21

The Bible tells us to love our neighbors

and also to love our enemies—

probably because generally they are the same people.

G. K. CHESTERTON

For the LORD your God is he that goeth with you, to fight for you against your enemies, to save you.   DEUTERONOMY 20:4

Thou preparest a table before me in the presence of mine enemies: thou anointest my head with oil; my cup runneth over.
                                                        PSALM 23:5

So that we may boldly say, The Lord is my helper, and I will not fear what man shall do unto me.   HEBREWS 13:6

That we should be saved from our enemies, and from the hand of all that hate us.   LUKE 1:71

Agree with thine adversary quickly, whiles thou art in the way with him; lest at any time the adversary deliver thee to the judge, and the judge deliver thee to the officer, and thou be cast into prison.
                                                      MATTHEW 5:25

That he would grant unto us, that we, being delivered out of the hand of our enemies, might serve him without fear. LUKE 1:74

Though I walk in the midst of trouble, thou wilt revive me: thou shalt stretch forth thine hand against the wrath of mine enemies, and thy right hand shall save me. PSALM 138:7

For in the time of trouble he shall hide me in his pavilion: in the secret of his tabernacle shall he hide me; he shall set me up upon a rock. And now shall mine head be lifted up above mine enemies round about me: therefore will I offer in his tabernacle sacrifices of joy; I will sing, yea, I will sing praises unto the LORD.

PSALM 27:5–6

And the LORD shall help them, and deliver them: he shall deliver them from the wicked, and save them, because they trust in him.

PSALM 37:40

If thine enemy be hungry, give him bread to eat; and if he be thirsty, give him water to drink: For thou shalt heap coals of fire upon his head, and the LORD shall reward thee.

PROVERBS 25:21–22

They that hate thee shall be clothed with shame; and the dwelling place of the wicked shall come to nought. JOB 8:22

For the rod of the wicked shall not rest upon the lot of the righteous; lest the righteous put forth their hands unto iniquity.

PSALM 125:3

His heart is established, he shall not be afraid, until he see his desire upon his enemies. PSALM 112:8

In famine he shall redeem thee from death: and in war from the power of the sword. JOB 5:20

Through God we shall do valiantly: for he it is that shall tread down our enemies.   PSALM 60:12

No weapon that is formed against thee shall prosper; and every tongue that shall rise against thee in judgment thou shalt condemn. This is the heritage of the servants of the LORD, and their righteousness is of me, saith the LORD.   ISAIAH 54:17

The LORD shall cause thine enemies that rise up against thee to be smitten before thy face: they shall come out against thee one way, and flee before thee seven ways.   DEUTERONOMY 28:7

If I make my enemy my friend,

have I not destroyed my enemies?

ABRAHAM LINCOLN

And shall not God avenge his own elect, which cry day and night unto him, though he bear long with them?   LUKE 18:7

Behold, they shall surely gather together, but not by me: whosoever shall gather together against thee shall fall for thy sake.
                                                        ISAIAH 54:15

But I will deliver thee in that day, saith the LORD: and thou shalt not be given into the hand of the men of whom thou art afraid. For I will surely deliver thee, and thou shalt not fall by the sword, but thy life shall be for a prey unto thee: because thou hast put thy trust in me, saith the LORD.   JEREMIAH 39:17–18

But the LORD your God ye shall fear; and he shall deliver you out of the hand of all your enemies.   2 KINGS 17:39

Ye that love the LORD, hate evil: he preserveth the souls of his saints; he delivereth them out of the hand of the wicked.

PSALM 97:10

And he answered, Fear not: for they that be with us are more than they that be with them.   2 KINGS 6:16

Behold, all they that were incensed against thee shall be ashamed and confounded: they shall be as nothing; and they that strive with thee shall perish. Thou shalt seek them, and shalt not find them, even them that contended with thee: they that war against thee shall be as nothing, and as a thing of nought.   ISAIAH 41:11–12

Be not afraid of sudden fear, neither of the desolation of the wicked, when it cometh. For the LORD shall be thy confidence, and shall keep thy foot from being taken.   PROVERBS 3:25–26

For I am with thee, and no man shall set on thee to hurt thee: for I have much people in this city.   ACTS 18:10

So that we may boldly say, The Lord is my helper, and I will not fear what man shall do unto me.   HEBREWS 13:6

ENVY

Seek not great things for yourselves in this world,
for if your garments be too long,
they will make you stumble;
and one staff helps a man in his journey,
when many in his hands at once hinders him.

WILLIAM BRIDGE

Neither shalt thou desire thy neighbour's wife, neither shalt thou covet thy neighbour's house, his field, or his manservant, or his maidservant, his ox, or his ass, or any thing that is thy neighbour's.

DEUTERONOMY 5:21

For where envying and strife is, there is confusion and every evil work.

JAMES 3:16

Do ye think that the scripture saith in vain, The spirit that dwelleth in us lusteth to envy?

JAMES 4:5

Let us not be desirous of vain glory, provoking one another, envying one another.   GALATIANS 5:26

For the wicked boasteth of his heart's desire, and blesseth the covetous, whom the LORD abhorreth.   PSALM 10:3

Envy thou not the oppressor, and choose none of his ways.
                                                          PROVERBS 3:31

A sound heart is the life of the flesh: but envy the rottenness of the bones.   PROVERBS 14:30

Wrath is cruel, and anger is outrageous; but who is able to stand before envy?   PROVERBS 27:4

Rest in the LORD, and wait patiently for him: fret not thyself because of him who prospereth in his way.   PSALM 37:7

Again, I considered all travail, and every right work, that for this a man is envied of his neighbour. This is also vanity and vexation of spirit.   ECCLESIASTES 4:4

Be not thou envious against evil men, neither desire to be with them.   PROVERBS 24:1

But if ye have bitter envying and strife in your hearts, glory not, and lie not against the truth.   JAMES 3:14

Let not thine heart envy sinners: but be thou in the fear of the LORD all the day long. For surely there is an end; and thine expectation shall not be cut off.   PROVERBS 23:17–18

And he said unto his disciples, Therefore I say unto you, Take no thought for your life, what ye shall eat; neither for the body, what ye shall put on. The life is more than meat, and the body is more than raiment.   LUKE 12:22–23

FAITH

Faith is not
the absence of questioning;
it is the presence of
action in the midst of
those questions.

WOODROW KROLL

It is written in the prophets, And they shall be all taught of God. Every man therefore that hath heard, and hath learned of the Father, cometh unto me.   JOHN 6:45

That Christ may dwell in your hearts by faith; that ye, being rooted and grounded in love, may be able to comprehend with all saints what is the breadth, and length, and depth, and height; and to know the love of Christ, which passeth knowledge, that ye might be filled with all the fulness of God.   EPHESIANS 3:17–19

Now faith is the substance of things hoped for, the evidence of things not seen. HEBREWS 11:1

Jesus said unto him, If thou canst believe, all things are possible to him that believeth. MARK 9:23

That your faith should not stand in the wisdom of men, but in the power of God. 1 CORINTHIANS 2:5

And the Lord said, If ye had faith as a grain of mustard seed, ye might say unto this sycamine tree, Be thou plucked up by the root, and be thou planted in the sea; and it should obey you.
LUKE 17:6

For we walk by faith, not by sight. 2 CORINTHIANS 5:7

Whom having not seen, ye love; in whom, though now ye see him not, yet believing, ye rejoice with joy unspeakable and full of glory.
1 PETER 1:8

As soon as Jesus heard the word that was spoken, he saith unto the ruler of the synagogue, Be not afraid, only believe. MARK 5:36

For ye are all the children of God by faith in Christ Jesus.
GALATIANS 3:26

And he said to the woman, Thy faith hath saved thee; go in peace.
LUKE 7:50

But as many as received him, to them gave he power to become the sons of God, even to them that believe on his name. JOHN 1:12

That if thou shalt confess with thy mouth the Lord Jesus, and shalt believe in thine heart that God hath raised him from the dead, thou shalt be saved. ROMANS 10:9

He that believeth and is baptized shall be saved; but he that believeth not shall be damned.   MARK 16:16

Let us draw near with a true heart in full assurance of faith, having our hearts sprinkled from an evil conscience, and our bodies washed with pure water.   HEBREWS 10:22

He that believeth on the Son of God hath the witness in himself: he that believeth not God hath made him a liar; because he believeth not the record that God gave of his Son.   1 JOHN 5:10

Where reason cannot wade there faith may swim.

THOMAS WATSON

Watch ye, stand fast in the faith, quit you like men, be strong.
          1 CORINTHIANS 16:13

Jesus saith unto her, Said I not unto thee, that, if thou wouldest believe, thou shouldest see the glory of God?   JOHN 11:40

The life which I now live in the flesh I live by the faith of the Son of God, who loved me, and gave himself for me.   GALATIANS 2:20

Jesus saith unto him, Thomas, because thou hast seen me, thou hast believed: blessed are they that have not seen, and yet have believed.   JOHN 20:29

And Jesus answering saith unto them, Have faith in God. For verily I say unto you, That whosoever shall say unto this mountain, Be thou removed, and be thou cast into the sea; and shall not doubt in his heart, but shall believe that those things which he saith shall come to pass; he shall have whatsoever he saith.   MARK 11:22–23

Jesus answered and said unto them, This is the work of God, that ye believe on him whom he hath sent. JOHN 6:29

As ye have therefore received Christ Jesus the Lord, so walk ye in him. COLOSSIANS 2:6–7

For by grace are ye saved through faith; and that not of yourselves: it is the gift of God. EPHESIANS 2:8

But without faith it is impossible to please him: for he that cometh to God must believe that he is, and that he is a rewarder of them that diligently seek him. HEBREWS 11:6

If any of you lack wisdom, let him ask of God, that giveth to all men liberally, and upbraideth not; and it shall be given him. But let him ask in faith, nothing wavering. For he that wavereth is like a wave of the sea driven with the wind and tossed. JAMES 1:5–6

But continue thou in the things which thou hast learned and hast been assured of, knowing of whom thou hast learned them; and that from a child thou hast known the holy scriptures, which are able to make thee wise unto salvation through faith which is in Christ Jesus. 2 TIMOTHY 3:14–15

Wherefore seeing we also are compassed about with so great a cloud of witnesses, let us lay aside every weight, and the sin which doth so easily beset us, and let us run with patience the race that is set before us, looking unto Jesus the author and finisher of our faith; who for the joy that was set before him endured the cross, despising the shame, and is set down at the right hand of the throne of God. HEBREWS 12:1–2

FAITHFULNESS OF GOD

*Your heavenly Father
is too good to be
unkind and too wise to
make mistakes.*

CHARLES H. SPURGEON

God is not a man, that he should lie; neither the son of man, that he should repent: hath he said, and shall he not do it? Or hath he spoken, and shall he not make it good?   NUMBERS 23:19

Blessed be the LORD, that hath given rest unto his people Israel, according to all that he promised: there hath not failed one word of all his good promise, which he promised by the hand of Moses his servant.   1 KINGS 8:56

If we believe not, yet he abideth faithful: he cannot deny himself.
    2 TIMOTHY 2:13

Know therefore that the LORD thy God, he is God, the faithful God, which keepeth covenant and mercy with them that love him and keep his commandments to a thousand generations.

DEUTERONOMY 7:9

And the heavens shall praise thy wonders, O LORD: thy faithfulness also in the congregation of the saints.   PSALM 89:5

In hope of eternal life, which God, that cannot lie, promised before the world began.   TITUS 1:2

(For the LORD thy God is a merciful God;) he will not forsake thee, neither destroy thee, nor forget the covenant of thy fathers which he sware unto them.   DEUTERONOMY 4:31

He hath remembered his covenant for ever, the word which he commanded to a thousand generations.   PSALM 105:8

Let us hold fast the profession of our faith without wavering; (for he is faithful that promised).   HEBREWS 10:23

The Lord is not slack concerning his promise, as some men count slackness; but is longsuffering to us-ward.   2 PETER 3:9

And they that know thy name will put their trust in thee: for thou, LORD, hast not forsaken them that seek thee.   PSALM 9:10

For ever, O LORD, thy word is settled in heaven. Thy faithfulness is unto all generations.   PSALM 119:89–90

Thy word is true from the beginning: and every one of thy righteous judgments endureth for ever.   PSALM 119:160

My covenant will I not break, nor alter the thing that is gone out of my lips.   PSALM 89:34

O LORD, thou art my God; I will exalt thee, I will praise thy name; for thou hast done wonderful things; thy counsels of old are faithfulness and truth.   ISAIAH 25:1

Faith looks straight to the command in order to

obey it and takes the promise for her support.

She pushes on her way, regardless of dangers.

Moses must go forward,

though the next step lead the people into the sea.

Whatever appearances may say to us,

it is by advancing in the narrow way of obedience

that we prove the truth of the promises,

and the faithfulness, wisdom, and power

of our promise-keeping God.

ROBERT C. CHAPMAN

FEAR

We fear men so much because we fear God so little.
One fear cures another.
When man's terror scares you,
turn your thoughts to the wrath of God.

WILLIAM GURNALL

And he said unto them, Why are ye so fearful? how is it that ye have no faith?   MARK 4:40

For I the LORD thy God will hold thy right hand, saying unto thee, Fear not; I will help thee.   ISAIAH 41:13

But whoso hearkeneth unto me shall dwell safely, and shall be quiet from fear of evil.   PROVERBS 1:33

And fear not them which kill the body, but are not able to kill the soul.   MATTHEW 10:28

Be not afraid of sudden fear, neither of the desolation of the wicked, when it cometh. For the LORD shall be thy confidence, and shall keep thy foot from being taken. PROVERBS 3:25–26

For God hath not given us the spirit of fear; but of power, and of love, and of a sound mind. 2 TIMOTHY 1:7

The wise man in the storm prays God,

not for safety from danger,

but for deliverance from fear.

RALPH WALDO EMERSON

The LORD shall give thee rest from thy sorrow, and from thy fear, and from the hard bondage wherein thou wast made to serve. ISAIAH 14:3

When thou liest down, thou shalt not be afraid: yea, thou shalt lie down, and thy sleep shall be sweet. PROVERBS 3:24

In righteousness shalt thou be established: thou shalt be far from oppression; for thou shalt not fear: and from terror; for it shall not come near thee. ISAIAH 54:14

For ye have not received the spirit of bondage again to fear; but ye have received the Spirit of adoption, whereby we cry, Abba, Father. ROMANS 8:15

I, even I, am he that comforteth you: who art thou, that thou shouldest be afraid of a man that shall die, and of the son of man which shall be made as grass. ISAIAH 51:12

So that we may boldly say, The Lord is my helper, and I will not fear what man shall do unto me.   HEBREWS 13:6

For the eyes of the Lord are over the righteous, and his ears are open unto their prayers: but the face of the Lord is against them that do evil. And who is he that will harm you, if ye be followers of that which is good? But and if ye suffer for righteousness' sake, happy are ye: and be not afraid of their terror, neither be troubled.   1 PETER 3:12–14

God is our refuge and strength, a very present help in trouble.
                                                                PSALM 46:1

The fear of man bringeth a snare: but whoso putteth his trust in the LORD shall be safe.   PROVERBS 29:25

He shall cover thee with his feathers, and under his wings shalt thou trust: his truth shall be thy shield and buckler. Thou shalt not be afraid for the terror by night; nor for the arrow that flieth by day; nor for the pestilence that walketh in darkness; nor for the destruction that wasteth at noonday.   PSALM 91:4–6

Fear not; for thou shalt not be ashamed: neither be thou confounded.
                                                                ISAIAH 54:4

When thou passest through the waters, I will be with thee; and through the rivers, they shall not overflow thee: when thou walkest through the fire, thou shalt not be burned; neither shall the flame kindle upon thee.   ISAIAH 43:2

Peace I leave with you, my peace I give unto you: not as the world giveth, give I unto you. Let not your heart be troubled, neither let it be afraid.   JOHN 14:27

Yea, though I walk through the valley of the shadow of death, I will fear no evil: for thou art with me; thy rod and thy staff they comfort me.   PSALM 23:4–5

FORGIVENESS

*Forgiveness is
the oil of relationships.*

JOSH MCDOWELL

For if ye forgive men their trespasses, your heavenly Father will also forgive you: But if ye forgive not men their trespasses, neither will your Father forgive your trespasses.   MATTHEW 6:14–15

The discretion of a man deferreth his anger; and it is his glory to pass over a transgression.   PROVERBS 19:11

Not rendering evil for evil, or railing for railing: but contrariwise blessing; knowing that ye are thereunto called, that ye should inherit a blessing.   1 PETER 3:9

And be ye kind one to another, tenderhearted, forgiving one another, even as God for Christ's sake hath forgiven you.   EPHESIANS 4:32

But I say unto you, That ye resist not evil: but whosoever shall smite thee on thy right cheek, turn to him the other also. And if any man will sue thee at the law, and take away thy coat, let him have thy cloke also. And whosoever shall compel thee to go a mile, go with him twain.   MATTHEW 5:39–41

Take heed to yourselves: If thy brother trespass against thee, rebuke him; and if he repent, forgive him. And if he trespass against thee seven times in a day, and seven times in a day turn again to thee, saying, I repent; thou shalt forgive him.   LUKE 17:3–4

"I can forgive but I cannot forget"

is only another way of saying,

"I will not forgive."

Forgiveness ought to be like a cancelled note—

torn in two and burned up,

so that it never can be shown against one.

HENRY WARD BEECHER

Then came Peter to him, and said, Lord, how oft shall my brother sin against me, and I forgive him? till seven times? Jesus saith unto him, I say not unto thee, Until seven times: but, Until seventy times seven.   MATTHEW 18:21–22

And forgive us our sins; for we also forgive every one that is indebted to us. And lead us not into temptation; but deliver us from evil.   LUKE 11:4

And when ye stand praying, forgive, if ye have ought against any: that your Father also which is in heaven may forgive you your trespasses. But if ye do not forgive, neither will your Father which is in heaven forgive your trespasses.   MARK 11:25–26

Forbearing one another, and forgiving one another, if any man have a quarrel against any: even as Christ forgave you, so also do ye.
                                                    COLOSSIANS 3:13

FRUITFULNESS

When we are engaged in His work,
we are very close to Christ.
We are expending our anxiety and affections
on the same objects on which His heart is set.

JAMES STALKER

And he shall be like a tree planted by the rivers of water, that bringeth forth his fruit in his season; his leaf also shall not wither; and whatsoever he doeth shall prosper. PSALM 1:3

They shall still bring forth fruit in old age; they shall be fat and flourishing. PSALM 92:14

For if these things be in you, and abound, they make you that ye shall neither be barren nor unfruitful in the knowledge of our Lord Jesus Christ. 2 PETER 1:8

I will be as the dew unto Israel: he shall grow as the lily, and cast forth his roots as Lebanon.   HOSEA 14:5

Therefore they shall come and sing in the height of Zion, and shall flow together to the goodness of the LORD, for wheat, and for wine, and for oil, and for the young of the flock and of the herd: and their soul shall be as a watered garden; and they shall not sorrow any more at all.   JEREMIAH 31:12

I am the true vine, and my father is the husbandman. Every branch in me that beareth not fruit he taketh away: and every branch that beareth fruit, he purgeth it, that it may bring forth more fruit. Now ye are clean through the word which I have spoken unto you. Abide in me, and I in you. As the branch cannot bear fruit of itself, except it abide in the vine; no more can ye, except ye abide in me. I am the vine, ye are the branches: He that abideth in me, and I in him, the same bringeth forth much fruit: for without me ye can do nothing.   JOHN 15:1–5

Herein is my Father glorified, that ye bear much fruit; so shall ye be my disciples.   JOHN 15:8

GENEROSITY

Give what you have.
To someone,
it may be better than
you dare to think.

HENRY WADSWORTH LONGFELLOW

Therefore when thou doest thine alms, do not sound a trumpet before thee, as the hypocrites do in the synagogues and in the streets, that they may have glory of men. Verily I say unto you, They have their reward. But when thou doest alms, let not thy left hand know what thy right hand doeth: That thine alms may be in secret: and thy Father which seeth in secret himself shall reward thee openly. MATTHEW 6:2–4

For the poor shall never cease out of the land: therefore I command thee, saying, Thou shalt open thine hand wide unto thy brother, to thy poor, and to thy needy, in thy land. DEUTERONOMY 15:11

And if thy brother be waxen poor, and fallen in decay with thee; then thou shalt relieve him: yea, though he be a stranger, or a sojourner; that he may live with thee.   LEVITICUS 25:35

If any man or woman that believeth have widows, let them relieve them, and let not the church be charged; that it may relieve them that are widows indeed.   1 TIMOTHY 5:16

Whatsoever I thankfully receive,

as a token of God's love to me,

I part with contentedly as a token of my love to Him.

THEOPHILUS GALE

If a brother or sister be naked, and destitute of daily food, and one of you say unto them, Depart in peace, be ye warmed and filled; notwithstanding ye give them not those things which are needful to the body; what doth it profit?   JAMES 2:15–16

Is it not to deal thy bread to the hungry, and that thou bring the poor that are cast out to thy house? when thou seest the naked, that thou cover him; and that thou hide not thyself from thine own flesh? Then shall thy light break forth as the morning, and thine health shall spring forth speedily: and thy righteousness shall go before thee; the glory of the LORD shall be thy reward.
          ISAIAH 58:7–8

Blessed is he that considereth the poor: the LORD will deliver him in time of trouble. The LORD will preserve him, and keep him alive; and he shall be blessed upon the earth: and thou wilt not deliver him unto the will of his enemies.   PSALM 41:1–2

Every man according as he purposeth in his heart, so let him give; not grudgingly, or of necessity: for God loveth a cheerful giver.

2 CORINTHIANS 9:7

He that despiseth his neighbour sinneth: but he that hath mercy on the poor, happy is he.

PROVERBS 14:21

And he saw also a certain poor widow casting in thither two mites. And he said, Of a truth I say unto you, that this poor widow hath cast in more than they all: For all these have of their abundance cast in unto the offerings of God: but she of her penury hath cast in all the living that she had.

LUKE 21:2–4

For whosoever shall give you a cup of water to drink in my name, because ye belong to Christ, verily I say unto you, he shall not lose his reward.

MARK 9:41

Then shall the King say unto them on his right hand, Come, ye blessed of my Father, inherit the kingdom prepared for you from the foundation of the world: For I was an hungred, and ye gave me meat: I was thirsty, and ye gave me drink: I was a stranger, and ye took me in: Naked, and ye clothed me: I was sick, and ye visited me: I was in prison, and ye came unto me. Then shall the righteous answer him, saying, Lord, when saw we thee an hungred, and fed thee? or thirsty, and gave thee drink? When saw we thee a stranger, and took thee in? or naked, and clothed thee? Or when saw we thee sick, or in prison, and came unto thee? And the King shall answer and say unto them, Verily I say unto you, Inasmuch as ye have done it unto one of the least of these my brethren, ye have done it unto me.

MATTHEW 25:34–40

Every man shall give as he is able, according to the blessing of the LORD thy God which he hath given thee.

DEUTERONOMY 16:17

He that hath pity upon the poor lendeth unto the LORD; and that which he hath given will he pay him again.

PROVERBS 19:17

Give, and it shall be given unto you; good measure, pressed down, and shaken together, and running over, shall men give into your bosom. For with the same measure that ye mete withal it shall be measured to you again.   LUKE 6:38

For ye know the grace of our Lord Jesus Christ, that, though he was rich, yet for your sakes he became poor, that ye through his poverty might be rich.   2 CORINTHIANS 8:9

He hath dispersed, he hath given to the poor; his righteousness endureth for ever; his horn shall be exalted with honour.
                                                        PSALM 112:9

When we come to the end of life,

the question will be, "How much have you given?"

not "How much have you gotten?"

GEORGE SWEETING

Charge them that are rich in this world, that they be not high-minded, nor trust in uncertain riches, but in the living God, who giveth us richly all things to enjoy; that they do good, that they be rich in good works, ready to distribute, willing to communicate.
                                                    1 TIMOTHY 6:17–18

I have shewed you all things, how that so labouring ye ought to support the weak, and to remember the words of the Lord Jesus, how he said, It is more blessed to give than to receive. ACTS 20:35

He answereth and saith unto them, He that hath two coats, let him impart to him that hath none; and he that hath meat, let him do likewise.   LUKE 3:11

But when thou makest a feast, call the poor, the maimed, the lame, the blind: and thou shalt be blessed; for they cannot recompense thee: for thou shalt be recompensed at the resurrection of the just.

LUKE 14:13–14

Withhold not good from them to whom it is due, when it is in the power of thine hand to do it. Say not unto thy neighbour, Go, and come again, and to morrow I will give; when thou hast it by thee.

PROVERBS 3:27–28

GOSSIP

If you want the truth to go round the world
you must hire an express train to pull it;
but if you want a lie to go round the world, it will fly;
it is as light as a feather, and a breath will carry it.
It is well said in the old proverb,
a lie will go round the world
while truth is putting its boots on.

CHARLES H. SPURGEON

Thou shalt not go up and down as a talebearer among thy people: neither shalt thou stand against the blood of thy neighbour: I am the LORD.   LEVITICUS 19:16

He that goeth about as a talebearer revealeth secrets: therefore meddle not with him that flattereth with his lips.   PROVERBS 20:19

The words of a talebearer are as wounds, and they go down into the innermost parts of the belly. PROVERBS 18:8

A talebearer revealeth secrets: but he that is of a faithful spirit concealeth the matter. PROVERBS 11:13

A froward man soweth strife: and a whisperer separateth chief friends. PROVERBS 16:28

Thy tongue deviseth mischiefs; like a sharp razor, working deceitfully. PSALM 52:2

All our words ought to be filled with

true sweetness and grace;

and this will be so if we mingle

the useful with the sweet.

JOHN CALVIN

Where no wood is, there the fire goeth out: so where there is no talebearer, the strife ceaseth. As coals are to burning coals, and wood to fire; so is a contentious man to kindle strife. The words of a talebearer are as wounds, and they go down into the innermost parts of the belly. PROVERBS 26:20–22

The north wind driveth away rain: so doth an angry countenance a backbiting tongue. PROVERBS 25:23

Keep thy tongue from evil, and thy lips from speaking guile. PSALM 34:13

GRATITUDE

For all the blessings of the year,
For all the friends we hold so dear,
For peace on earth, both far and near,
We thank Thee, Lord.

For life and health, those common things,
Which every day and hour brings,
For home, where our affection clings,
We thank Thee, Lord.

For love of Thine, which never tired,
Which all our better thought inspires,
And warms our lives with heavenly fires,
We thank Thee, Lord.

ALBERT H. HUTCHINSON

I will praise thee, O LORD, with my whole heart; I will shew forth all thy marvellous works. I will be glad and rejoice in thee: I will sing praise to thy name, O thou most High.   PSALM 9:1–2

In every thing give thanks: for this is the will of God in Christ Jesus concerning you.   1 THESSALONIANS 5:18

Blessed be the Lord, that hath given rest unto his people Israel, according to all that he promised: there hath not failed one word of all his good promise, which he promised by the hand of Moses his servant.   1 KINGS 8:56

That I may publish with the voice of thanksgiving, and tell of all thy wondrous works.   PSALM 26:7

O LORD, thou hast brought up my soul from the grave: thou hast kept me alive, that I should not go down to the pit.   PSALM 30:3

I thank thee, and praise thee, O thou God of my fathers, who hast given me wisdom and might, and hast made known unto me now what we desired of thee: for thou hast now made known unto us the king's matter.   DANIEL 2:23

Thou hast turned for me my mourning into dancing: thou hast put off my sackcloth, and girded me with gladness; to the end that my glory may sing praise to thee, and not be silent. O LORD my God, I will give thanks unto thee for ever.   PSALM 30:11–12

And he took the seven loaves and the fishes, and gave thanks, and brake them, and gave to his disciples, and the disciples to the multitude.   MATTHEW 15:36

It is a good thing to give thanks unto the LORD, and to sing praises unto thy name, O most High: To shew forth thy lovingkindness in the morning, and thy faithfulness every night.   PSALM 92:1–2

Blessed be the LORD, who daily loadeth us with benefits, even the God of our salvation. Selah.   PSALM 68:19

And they, continuing daily with one accord in the temple, and breaking bread from house to house, did eat their meat with gladness and singleness of heart, praising God, and having favour with all the people. And the Lord added to the church daily such as should be saved.   ACTS 2:46–47

I will mention the lovingkindnesses of the LORD, and the praises of the LORD, according to all that the LORD hath bestowed on us, and the great goodness toward the house of Israel, which he hath bestowed on them according to his mercies, and according to the multitude of his lovingkindnesses.   ISAIAH 63:7

We have been a most favored people.

We ought to be a most grateful people.

CALVIN COOLIDGE

Many, O LORD my God, are thy wonderful works which thou hast done, and thy thoughts which are to us-ward: they cannot be reckoned up in order unto thee: if I would declare and speak of them, they are more than can be numbered.   PSALM 40:5

O give thanks unto the LORD; for he is good: for his mercy endureth for ever.   PSALM 136:1

Giving thanks always for all things unto God and the Father in the name of our Lord Jesus Christ.   EPHESIANS 5:20

GUIDANCE

He that won't be counselled
can't be helped.

BENJAMIN FRANKLIN

Now no chastening for the present seemeth to be joyous, but grievous: nevertheless afterward it yieldeth the peaceable fruit of righteousness unto them which are exercised thereby.

HEBREWS 12:11

For unto us a child is born, unto us a son is given: and the government shall be upon his shoulder: and his name shall be called Wonderful, Counsellor, The mighty God, The everlasting Father, The Prince of Peace.

ISAIAH 9:6

And thine ears shall hear a word behind thee, saying, This is the way, walk ye in it, when ye turn to the right hand, and when ye turn to the left.

ISAIAH 30:21

Hear counsel, and receive instruction, that thou mayest be wise in thy latter end.   PROVERBS 19:20

Howbeit when he, the Spirit of truth, is come, he will guide you into all truth: for he shall not speak of himself; but whatsoever he shall hear, that shall he speak: and he will shew you things to come.
                                                                      JOHN 16:13

Give instruction to a wise man, and he will be yet wiser: teach a just man, and he will increase in learning.   PROVERBS 9:9

To what greater inspiration and counsel can we turn

than to the imperishable truth to be found

in this treasure house, the Bible?

QUEEN ELIZABETH II

The way of a fool is right in his own eyes: but he that hearkeneth unto counsel is wise.   PROVERBS 12:15

Ointment and perfume rejoice the heart: so doth the sweetness of a man's friend by hearty counsel.   PROVERBS 27:9

Without counsel purposes are disappointed: but in the multitude of counsellors they are established.   PROVERBS 15:22

A wise man will hear, and will increase learning; and a man of understanding shall attain unto wise counsels.   PROVERBS 1:5

Where no counsel is, the people fall: but in the multitude of counsellors there is safety.   PROVERBS 11:14

For this God is our God for ever and ever: he will be our guide even unto death.   PSALM 48:14

A man's heart deviseth his way: but the LORD directeth his steps.
PROVERBS 16:9

The steps of a good man are ordered by the LORD: and he delighteth in his way.   PSALM 37:23

For his God doth instruct him to discretion, and doth teach him.
ISAIAH 28:26

In all thy ways acknowledge him, and he shall direct thy paths.
PROVERBS 3:6

And I will bring the blind by a way that they knew not; I will lead them in the paths that they have not known: I will make darkness light before them, and crooked things straight. These things will I do unto them, and not forsake them.   ISAIAH 42:16

Brethren, if a man be overtaken in a fault, ye which are spiritual, restore such an one in the spirit of meekness; considering thyself, lest thou also be tempted.   GALATIANS 6:1

And all thy children shall be taught of the LORD; and great shall be the peace of thy children.   ISAIAH 54:13

GUILT

If we confess our sins,
he is faithful and just to forgive us our sins,
and to cleanse us from all unrighteousness.

1 JOHN 1:9

Therefore if any man be in Christ, he is a new creature: old things are passed away; behold, all things are become new.

2 CORINTHIANS 5:17

For the Lord your God is gracious and merciful, and will not turn away his face from you, if ye return unto him.   2 CHRONICLES 30:9

As far as the east is from the west, so far hath he removed our transgressions from us.   PSALM 103:12

For if our heart condemn us, God is greater than our heart, and knoweth all things.   1 JOHN 3:20

Let the wicked forsake his way, and the unrighteous man his thoughts: and let him return unto the LORD, and he will have mercy upon him; and to our God, for he will abundantly pardon.

ISAIAH 55:7

For I will be merciful to their unrighteousness, and their sins and their iniquities will I remember no more.
HEBREWS 8:12

For I will forgive their iniquity, and I will remember their sin no more.
JEREMIAH 31:34

And I will cleanse them from all their iniquity, whereby they have sinned against me; and I will pardon all their iniquities, whereby they have sinned, and whereby they have transgressed against me.

JEREMIAH 33:8

I write unto you, little children, because your sins are forgiven you for his name's sake.
1 JOHN 2:12

I, even I, am he that blotteth out thy transgressions for mine own sake, and will not remember thy sins.
ISAIAH 43:25

But if we walk in the light, as he is in the light, we have fellowship one with another, and the blood of Jesus Christ his Son cleanseth us from all sin.
1 JOHN 1:7

HONESTY

And he that
does one fault at first
and lies to hide it
makes it two.

ISAAC WATTS

Ye shall do no unrighteousness in judgment, in meteyard, in weight, or in measure. Just balances, just weights, a just ephah, and a just hin, shall ye have: I am the LORD your God, which brought you out of the land of Egypt. LEVITICUS 19:35–36

Thou knowest the commandments, Do not commit adultery, Do not kill, Do not steal, Do not bear false witness, Defraud not, Honour thy father and mother. MARK 10:19

Pray for us: for we trust we have a good conscience, in all things willing to live honestly. HEBREWS 13:18

Providing for honest things, not only in the sight of the Lord, but also in the sight of men. 2 CORINTHIANS 8:21

And as ye would that men should do to you, do ye also to them likewise. LUKE 6:31

Ye shall not steal, neither deal falsely, neither lie one to another. LEVITICUS 19:11

And herein do I exercise myself, to have always a conscience void of offence toward God, and toward men. ACTS 24:16

He that walketh righteously, and speaketh uprightly; he that despiseth the gain of oppressions, that shaketh his hands from holding of bribes, that stoppeth his ears from hearing of blood, and shutteth his eyes from seeing evil; he shall dwell on high: his place of defence shall be the munitions of rocks: bread shall be given him; his waters shall be sure. ISAIAH 33:15–16

Therefore all things whatsoever ye would that men should do to you, do ye even so to them: for this is the law and the prophets. MATTHEW 7:12

Then came also publicans to be baptized, and said unto him, Master, what shall we do? And he said unto them, Exact no more than that which is appointed you. LUKE 3:12–13

Lie not one to another, seeing that ye have put off the old man with his deeds; and have put on the new man, which is renewed in knowledge after the image of him that created him. COLOSSIANS 3:9–10

Servants, obey in all things your masters according to the flesh; not with eyeservice, as menpleasers; but in singleness of heart, fearing God. COLOSSIANS 3:22

Who shall ascend into the hill of the LORD? or who shall stand in his holy place? He that hath clean hands, and a pure heart; who hath not lifted up his soul unto vanity, nor sworn deceitfully.

PSALM 24:3–4

Receive us; we have wronged no man, we have corrupted no man, we have defrauded no man.   2 CORINTHIANS 7:2

A false balance is abomination to the LORD: but a just weight is his delight.   PROVERBS 11:1

In our manner of speech, our plans of living,

our dealings with others, our conduct and walk

in the church and out of it—

all should be done as becomes the gospel

(Philippians 1:27).

ALBERT BARNES

And if thou sell aught unto thy neighbour, or buyest aught of thy neighbour's hand, ye shall not oppress one another.

LEVITICUS 25:14

Are there yet the treasures of wickedness in the house of the wicked, and the scant measure that is abominable? Shall I count them pure with the wicked balances, and with the bag of deceitful weights? For the rich men thereof are full of violence, and the inhabitants thereof have spoken lies, and their tongue is deceitful in their mouth.   MICAH 6:10–12

My righteousness I hold fast, and will not let it go: my heart shall not reproach me so long as I live. JOB 27:6

The wicked borroweth, and payeth not again: but the righteous sheweth mercy, and giveth. PSALM 37:21

But thou shalt have a perfect and just weight, a perfect and just measure shalt thou have: that thy days may be lengthened in the land which the LORD thy God giveth thee. For all that do such things, and all that do unrighteously, are an abomination unto the LORD thy God. DEUTERONOMY 25:15–16

That no man go beyond and defraud his brother in any matter: because that the Lord is the avenger of all such, as we also have forewarned you and testified. For God hath not called us unto uncleanness, but unto holiness. 1 THESSALONIANS 4:6–7

Withhold not good from them to whom it is due, when it is in the power of thine hand to do it. PROVERBS 3:27

Better is a little with righteousness than great revenues without right. PROVERBS 16:8

HOPE

*Everything that is
done in the world
is done by hope.*

MARTIN LUTHER

In hope of eternal life, which God, that cannot lie, promised before the world began.   TITUS 1:2

But Christ as a son over his own house; whose house are we, if we hold fast the confidence and the rejoicing of the hope firm unto the end.   HEBREWS 3:6

That by two immutable things, in which it was impossible for God to lie, we might have a strong consolation, who have fled for refuge to lay hold upon the hope set before us: Which hope we have as an anchor of the soul, both sure and stedfast, and which entereth into that within the veil.   HEBREWS 6:18–19

And hope maketh not ashamed; because the love of God is shed abroad in our hearts by the Holy Ghost which is given unto us.

ROMANS 5:5

Blessed is the man that trusteth in the LORD, and whose hope the LORD is.

JEREMIAH 17:7

Now the God of hope fill you with all joy and peace in believing, that ye may abound in hope, through the power of the Holy Ghost.

ROMANS 15:13

To whom God would make known what is the riches of the glory of this mystery among the Gentiles; which is Christ in you, the hope of glory.

COLOSSIANS 1:27

Who by him do believe in God, that raised him up from the dead, and gave him glory; that your faith and hope might be in God.

1 PETER 1:21

It is good that a man should both hope and quietly wait for the salvation of the LORD.

LAMENTATIONS 3:26

Who against hope believed in hope, that he might become the father of many nations, according to that which was spoken, So shall thy seed be.

ROMANS 4:18

But I will hope continually, and will yet praise thee more and more.

PSALM 71:14

There is one body, and one Spirit, even as ye are called in one hope of your calling.

EPHESIANS 4:4

For we are saved by hope: but hope that is seen is not hope: for what a man seeth, why doth he yet hope for? But if we hope for that we see not, then do we with patience wait for it.

ROMANS 8:24–25

LORD, I have hoped for thy salvation, and done thy commandments.
PSALM 119:166

According to my earnest expectation and my hope, that in nothing I shall be ashamed, but that with all boldness, as always, so
now also Christ shall be magnified in my body, whether it be by
life, or by death.   PHILIPPIANS 1:20

Why art thou cast down, O my soul? and why art thou disquieted
within me? hope thou in God: for I shall yet praise him, who is the
health of my countenance, and my God.   PSALM 42:11

Hope means hoping when things are hopeless,

or it is no virtue at all. . . .

As long as matters are really hopeful,

hope is mere flattery or platitude;

it is only when everything is hopeless

that hope begins to be a strength.

G. K. CHESTERTON

The eyes of your understanding being enlightened; that ye may
know what is the hope of his calling, and what the riches of the
glory of his inheritance in the saints.   EPHESIANS 1:18

Wherefore gird up the loins of your mind, be sober, and hope to
the end for the grace that is to be brought unto you at the revelation of Jesus Christ.   1 PETER 1:13

For the hope which is laid up for you in heaven, whereof ye heard before in the word of the truth of the gospel.   COLOSSIANS 1:5

Now faith is the substance of things hoped for, the evidence of things not seen.   HEBREWS 11:1

Hope itself is like a star—

not to be seen in the sunshine of prosperity

and only to be discovered in the night of adversity.

CHARLES H. SPURGEON

For the needy shall not alway be forgotten: the expectation of the poor shall not perish for ever.   PSALM 9:18

For we through the Spirit wait for the hope of righteousness by faith.   GALATIANS 5:5

Be of good courage, and he shall strengthen your heart, all ye that hope in the LORD.   PSALM 31:24

For thou art my hope, O LORD God: thou art my trust from my youth.   PSALM 71:5

Blessed be the God and Father of our Lord Jesus Christ, which according to his abundant mercy hath begotten us again unto a lively hope by the resurrection of Jesus Christ from the dead.
    1 PETER 1:3

HOSPITALITY

How far you go in life depends
on your being tender with the young,
compassionate with the aged,
sympathetic with the striving,
and tolerant of the weak and strong.
Because someday in your life
you will have been all of these.

GEORGE WASHINGTON CARVER

Use hospitality one to another without grudging. As every man hath received the gift, even so minister the same one to another, as good stewards of the manifold grace of God.   1 PETER 4:9–10

If a brother or sister be naked, and destitute of daily food, and one of you say unto them, Depart in peace, be ye warmed and filled; notwithstanding ye give them not those things which are needful to the body; what doth it profit?   JAMES 2:15–16

For whosoever shall give you a cup of water to drink in my name, because ye belong to Christ, verily I say unto you, he shall not lose his reward. MARK 9:41

I have shewed you all things, how that so labouring ye ought to support the weak, and to remember the words of the Lord Jesus, how he said, It is more blessed to give than to receive. ACTS 20:35

Kindness is the language

which the deaf can hear

and the blind can see.

MARK TWAIN

But whoso hath this world's good, and seeth his brother have need, and shutteth up his bowels of compassion from him, how dwelleth the love of God in him? 1 JOHN 3:17

And the King shall answer and say unto them, Verily I say unto you, Inasmuch as ye have done it unto one of the least of these my brethren, ye have done it unto me. MATTHEW 25:40

Be not forgetful to entertain strangers: for thereby some have entertained angels unawares. HEBREWS 13:2

For I mean not that other men be eased, and ye burdened: but by an equality, that now at this time your abundance may be a supply for their want, that their abundance also may be a supply for your want: that there may be equality. 2 CORINTHIANS 8:13–14

Distributing to the necessity of saints; given to hospitality. ROMANS 12:13

HUMILITY

If I appear to be great in their eyes,
the Lord is most graciously helping me to see
how absolutely nothing I am without Him
and helping me to keep little in my own eyes.
He does use me. But I'm so concerned that He
uses me and that it is not of me the work is done.
The ax cannot boast of the trees it has cut down.
It could do nothing but for the woodsman.
He made it, he sharpened it, he used it.
The moment he throws it aside it becomes only one iron.
Oh, that I may never lose sight of this.
The spiritual leader of today is in all probability
one who yesterday expressed his humility
by working gladly and faithfully in second place.

SAMUEL LOGAN BRENGLE

Whosoever therefore shall humble himself as this little child, the same is greatest in the kingdom of heaven. MATTHEW 18:4

When men are cast down, then thou shalt say, There is lifting up; and he shall save the humble person. JOB 22:29

LORD, my heart is not haughty, nor mine eyes lofty: neither do I exercise myself in great matters, or in things too high for me. PSALM 131:1

By humility and the fear of the LORD are riches, and honour, and life. PROVERBS 22:4

But he giveth more grace. Wherefore he saith, God resisteth the proud, but giveth grace unto the humble. JAMES 4:6

Blessed are the poor in spirit: for theirs is the kingdom of heaven. MATTHEW 5:3

LORD, thou hast heard the desire of the humble: thou wilt prepare their heart, thou wilt cause thine ear to hear. PSALM 10:17

The fear of the LORD is the instruction of wisdom; and before honour is humility. PROVERBS 15:33

Yea, all of you be subject one to another, and be clothed with humility: for God resisteth the proud, and giveth grace to the humble. Humble yourselves therefore under the mighty hand of God, that he may exalt you in due time. 1 PETER 5:5–6

And whosoever shall exalt himself shall be abased; and he that shall humble himself shall be exalted. MATTHEW 23:12

Humble yourselves in the sight of the Lord, and he shall lift you up. JAMES 4:10

But made himself of no reputation, and took upon him the form of a servant, and was made in the likeness of men: And being found in fashion as a man, he humbled himself, and became obedient unto death, even the death of the cross. Wherefore God also hath highly exalted him, and given him a name which is above every name.   PHILIPPIANS 2:7–9

Surely he scorneth the scorners: but he giveth grace unto the lowly.
                                                         PROVERBS 3:34

Though the LORD be high, yet hath he respect unto the lowly: but the proud he knoweth afar off.   PSALM 138:6

No man is great if

he thinks he is.

WILL ROGERS

When he maketh inquisition for blood, he remembereth them: he forgetteth not the cry of the humble.   PSALM 9:12

Better it is to be of an humble spirit with the lowly, than to divide the spoil with the proud.   PROVERBS 16:19

For thus saith the high and lofty One that inhabiteth eternity, whose name is Holy; I dwell in the high and holy place, with him also that is of a contrite and humble spirit, to revive the spirit of the humble, and to revive the heart of the contrite ones.   ISAIAH 57:15

Let no man deceive himself. If any man among you seemeth to be wise in this world, let him become a fool, that he may be wise.
                                                     1 CORINTHIANS 3:18

When pride cometh, then cometh shame: but with the lowly is wisdom. PROVERBS 11:2

Let another man praise thee, and not thine own mouth; a stranger, and not thine own lips. PROVERBS 27:2

Be not rash with thy mouth, and let not thine heart be hasty to utter any thing before God: for God is in heaven, and thou upon earth: therefore let thy words be few. ECCLESIASTES 5:2

A man's pride shall bring him low: but honour shall uphold the humble in spirit. PROVERBS 29:23

Boast not thyself of tomorrow; for thou knowest not what a day may bring forth. PROVERBS 27:1

Be not wise in your own conceits. ROMANS 12:16

If I must needs glory, I will glory of the things which concern mine infirmities. 2 CORINTHIANS 11:30

Shall the ax boast itself against him that heweth therewith? or shall the saw magnify itself against him that shaketh it? as if the rod should shake itself against them that lift it up, or as if the staff should lift up itself, as if it were no wood. ISAIAH 10:15

And base things of the world, and things which are despised, hath God chosen, yea, and things which are not, to bring to nought things that are: that no flesh should glory in his presence.
1 CORINTHIANS 1:28–29

Even so the tongue is a little member, and boasteth great things. Behold, how great a matter a little fire kindleth! JAMES 3:5

JOY

Do not let
your happiness depend on
something you may lose. . .
only [upon] the Beloved
who will never pass away.

C. S. LEWIS

And the angel said unto them, Fear not: for, behold, I bring you good tidings of great joy, which shall be to all people.   LUKE 2:10

The LORD is my strength and my shield; my heart trusted in him, and I am helped: therefore my heart greatly rejoiceth; and with my song will I praise him.   PSALM 28:7

Rejoice ye in that day, and leap for joy: for, behold, your reward is great in heaven: for in the like manner did their fathers unto the prophets.   LUKE 6:23

Rejoice in the Lord always: and again I say, Rejoice.

PHILIPPIANS 4:4

Is any merry? let him sing psalms.   James 5:13

I will see you again, and your heart shall rejoice, and your joy no man taketh from you. . . . Hitherto have ye asked nothing in my name: ask, and ye shall receive, that your joy may be full.   JOHN 16:22, 24

Be glad in the LORD, and rejoice, ye righteous: and shout for joy, all ye that are upright in heart.   PSALM 32:11

In the transgression of an evil man there is a snare: but the righteous doth sing and rejoice.   PROVERBS 29:6

As sorrowful, yet alway rejoicing; as poor, yet making many rich; as having nothing, and yet possessing all things.   2 CORINTHIANS 6:10

My lips shall greatly rejoice when I sing unto thee; and my soul, which thou hast redeemed.   PSALM 71:23

Therefore the redeemed of the LORD shall return, and come with singing unto Zion; and everlasting joy shall be upon their head: they shall obtain gladness and joy; and sorrow and mourning shall flee away.   ISAIAH 51:11

A merry heart doeth good like a medicine: but a broken spirit drieth the bones.   PROVERBS 17:22

Make a joyful noise unto the LORD, all ye lands. Serve the LORD with gladness: come before his presence with singing.

PSALM 100:1–2

All the days of the afflicted are evil: but he that is of a merry heart hath a continual feast.   PROVERBS 15:15

Weeping may endure for a night, but joy cometh in the morning.

PSALM 30:5

Let all those that seek thee rejoice and be glad in thee: let such as love thy salvation say continually, The LORD be magnified.

PSALM 40:16

When I think of God,

my heart is so filled with joy

that the notes fly off as from a spindle.

JOSEPH HAYDN

For our heart shall rejoice in him, because we have trusted in his holy name.

PSALM 33:21

Speaking to yourselves in psalms and hymns and spiritual songs, singing and making melody in your heart to the Lord.

EPHESIANS 5:19

I will greatly rejoice in the LORD, my soul shall be joyful in my God; for he hath clothed me with the garments of salvation, he hath covered me with the robe of righteousness, as a bridegroom decketh himself with ornaments, and as a bride adorneth herself with her jewels.

ISAIAH 61:10

Thou hast put gladness in my heart, more than in the time that their corn and their wine increased.

PSALM 4:7

These things have I spoken unto you, that my joy might remain in you, and that your joy might be full.

JOHN 15:11

For ye shall go out with joy, and be led forth with peace: the mountains and the hills shall break forth before you into singing, and all the trees of the field shall clap their hands.   ISAIAH 55:12

Blessed is the people that know the joyful sound: they shall walk, O LORD, in the light of thy countenance. In thy name shall they rejoice all the day: in thy righteousness shall they be exalted.
                                                          PSALM 89:15–16

They that sow in tears shall reap in joy. He that goeth forth and weepeth, bearing precious seed, shall doubtless come again with rejoicing, bringing his sheaves with him.   PSALM 126:5–6

For then shalt thou have thy delight in the Almighty, and shalt lift up thy face unto God.   JOB 22:26

Yet I will rejoice in the LORD, I will joy in the God of my salvation.
                                                          HABAKKUK 3:18

Whom having not seen, ye love; in whom, though now ye see him not, yet believing, ye rejoice with joy unspeakable and full of glory.
                                                          1 PETER 1:8

Then he said unto them, Go your way, eat the fat, and drink the sweet, and send portions unto them for whom nothing is prepared: for this day is holy unto our LORD: neither be ye sorry; for the joy of the LORD is your strength.   NEHEMIAH 8:10

And thou shalt rejoice in the LORD, and shalt glory in the Holy One of Israel.   ISAIAH 41:16

The righteous shall be glad in the LORD, and shall trust in him; and all the upright in heart shall glory.   PSALM 64:10

But let the righteous be glad; let them rejoice before God: yea, let them exceedingly rejoice.   PSALM 68:3

We may sing beforehand, even in our winter storm,

in the expectation of a summer sun

at the turn of the year;

no created powers can mar our Lord Jesus' music,

nor spill our song of joy.

Let us then be glad and rejoice

in the salvation of our Lord. . . .

SAMUEL RUTHERFORD

JUSTICE

*We are always
looking for justice,
yet the essence of
the teaching of
the Sermon on the Mount is—
Never look for justice,
but never cease to give it.*

OSWALD CHAMBERS

Thou shalt not defraud thy neighbour, neither rob him: the wages of him that is hired shall not abide with thee all night until the morning. Thou shalt not curse the deaf, nor put a stumblingblock before the blind, but shalt fear thy God: I am the LORD. Ye shall do no unrighteousness in judgment: thou shalt not respect the person of the poor, nor honour the person of the mighty: but in righteousness shalt thou judge thy neighbour.   LEVITICUS 19:13–15

Thou shalt not raise a false report: put not thine hand with the wicked to be an unrighteous witness. Thou shalt not follow a multitude to do evil; neither shalt thou speak in a cause to decline after many to wrest judgment: Neither shalt thou countenance a poor man in his cause.   EXODUS 23:1–3

Doth our law judge any man, before it hear him, and know what he doeth?   JOHN 7:51

If there be a controversy between men, and they come unto judgment, that the judges may judge them; then they shall justify the righteous, and condemn the wicked.   DEUTERONOMY 25:1

Power at its best is love

implementing the demands of justice.

Justice at its best is love

correcting everything that stands against love.

MARTIN LUTHER KING JR.

How long will ye judge unjustly, and accept the persons of the wicked? Selah. Defend the poor and fatherless: do justice to the afflicted and needy. Deliver the poor and needy: rid them out of the hand of the wicked.   PSALM 82:2–4

And moreover I saw under the sun the place of judgment, that wickedness was there; and the place of righteousness, that iniquity was there. I said in mine heart, God shall judge the righteous and the wicked: for there is a time there for every purpose and for every work.   ECCLESIASTES 3:16–17

But if ye had known what this meaneth, I will have mercy, and not sacrifice, ye would not have condemned the guiltless.

MATTHEW 12:7

Thus saith the LORD, Keep ye judgment, and do justice: for my salvation is near to come, and my righteousness to be revealed.

ISAIAH 56:1

Thus saith the LORD; Execute ye judgment and righteousness, and deliver the spoiled out of the hand of the oppressor: and do no wrong, do no violence to the stranger, the fatherless, nor the widow, neither shed innocent blood in this place.   JEREMIAH 22:3

That no man go beyond and defraud his brother in any matter: because that the Lord is the avenger of all such, as we also have forewarned you and testified. For God hath not called us unto uncleanness, but unto holiness.   1 THESSALONIANS 4:6–7

To turn aside the right of a man before the face of the most High, to subvert a man in his cause, the LORD approveth not.

LAMENTATIONS 3:35–36

Judge not according to the appearance, but judge righteous judgment.

JOHN 7:24

He that justifieth the wicked, and he that condemneth the just, even they both are abomination to the LORD.   PROVERBS 17:15

Thou shalt not wrest the judgment of thy poor in his cause. Keep thee far from a false matter; and the innocent and righteous slay thou not: for I will not justify the wicked. And thou shalt take no gift: for the gift blindeth the wise, and perverteth the words of the righteous.   EXODUS 23:6–8

Learn to do well; seek judgment, relieve the oppressed, judge the fatherless, plead for the widow.   ISAIAH 1:17

LAZINESS

*Never leave that
till tomorrow which
you can do today.*

BENJAMIN FRANKLIN

Labour not for the meat which perisheth, but for that meat which endureth unto everlasting life, which the Son of man shall give unto you: for him hath God the Father sealed.   JOHN 6:27

Whatsoever is commanded by the God of heaven, let it be diligently done for the house of the God of heaven: for why should there be wrath against the realm of the king and his sons?

EZRA 7:23

Or he that exhorteth, on exhortation: he that giveth, let him do it with simplicity; he that ruleth, with diligence; he that sheweth mercy, with cheerfulness.   ROMANS 12:8

Wherefore the rather, brethren, give diligence to make your calling and election sure: for if ye do these things, ye shall never fall: For so an entrance shall be ministered unto you abundantly into the everlasting kingdom of our Lord and Saviour Jesus Christ.

2 PETER 1:10–11

Behold that which I have seen: it is good and comely for one to eat and to drink, and to enjoy the good of all his labour that he taketh under the sun all the days of his life, which God giveth him: for it is his portion. Every man also to whom God hath given riches and wealth, and hath given him power to eat thereof, and to take his portion, and to rejoice in his labour; this is the gift of God.

ECCLESIASTES 5:18–19

I must work the works of him that sent me, while it is day: the night cometh, when no man can work. JOHN 9:4

The thoughts of the diligent tend only to plenteousness; but of every one that is hasty only to want. PROVERBS 21:5

Wherefore, beloved, seeing that ye look for such things, be diligent that ye may be found of him in peace, without spot, and blameless. 2 PETER 3:14

And let us not be weary in well doing: for in due season we shall reap, if we faint not. GALATIANS 6:9

Therefore, my beloved brethren, be ye stedfast, unmoveable, always abounding in the work of the Lord, forasmuch as ye know that your labour is not in vain in the Lord. 1 CORINTHIANS 15:58

And beside this, giving all diligence, add to your faith virtue; and to virtue knowledge. 2 PETER 1:5

Not slothful in business; fervent in spirit; serving the Lord.

ROMANS 12:11

And that ye study to be quiet, and to do your own business, and to work with your own hands, as we commanded you; that ye may walk honestly toward them that are without, and that ye may have lack of nothing.   1 THESSALONIANS 4:11–12

He that tilleth his land shall have plenty of bread: but he that followeth after vain persons shall have poverty enough.
                                          PROVERBS 28:19

Dost thou love life?

Then do not squander time;

for that's the stuff life is made of.

BENJAMIN FRANKLIN

The soul of the sluggard desireth, and hath nothing: but the soul of the diligent shall be made fat.   PROVERBS 13:4

He becometh poor that dealeth with a slack hand: but the hand of the diligent maketh rich. He that gathereth in summer is a wise son: but he that sleepeth in harvest is a son that causeth shame.
                                          PROVERBS 10:4–5

Much food is in the tillage of the poor: but there is that is destroyed for want of judgment.   PROVERBS 13:23

The husbandman that laboureth must be first partaker of the fruits.   2 TIMOTHY 2:6

Love not sleep, lest thou come to poverty; open thine eyes, and thou shalt be satisfied with bread.   PROVERBS 20:13

For even when we were with you, this we commanded you, that if any would not work, neither should he eat. For we hear that there are some which walk among you disorderly, working not at all, but are busybodies. Now them that are such we command and exhort by our Lord Jesus Christ, that with quietness they work, and eat their own bread.   2 THESSALONIANS 3:10–12

I went by the field of the slothful, and by the vineyard of the man void of understanding; and, lo, it was all grown over with thorns, and nettles had covered the face thereof, and the stone wall thereof was broken down. Then I saw, and considered it well: I looked upon it, and received instruction. Yet a little sleep, a little slumber, a little folding of the hands to sleep: So shall thy poverty come as one that travelleth; and thy want as an armed man.

PROVERBS 24:30–34

The way of the slothful man is as an hedge of thorns: but the way of the righteous is made plain.   PROVERBS 15:19

Be thou diligent to know the state of thy flocks, and look well to thy herds.   PROVERBS 27:23

The hand of the diligent shall bear rule: but the slothful shall be under tribute.   PROVERBS 12:24

Let him that stole steal no more: but rather let him labour, working with his hands the thing which is good, that he may have to give to him that needeth.   EPHESIANS 4:28

He that tilleth his land shall be satisfied with bread: but he that followeth vain persons is void of understanding.   PROVERBS 12:11

And thou shalt have goats' milk enough for thy food, for the food of thy household, and for the maintenance for thy maidens.

PROVERBS 27:27

LEADERSHIP

Leadership:
The art of getting someone else to do
something you want done
because he wants to do it.

DWIGHT D. EISENHOWER

Feed the flock of God which is among you, taking the oversight thereof, not by constraint, but willingly; not for filthy lucre, but of a ready mind; neither as being lords over God's heritage, but being ensamples to the flock. And when the chief Shepherd shall appear, ye shall receive a crown of glory that fadeth not away.

1 PETER 5:2–4

And they that have believing masters, let them not despise them, because they are brethren; but rather do them service, because they are faithful and beloved, partakers of the benefit. These things teach and exhort.

1 TIMOTHY 6:2

But thou, O man of God, flee these things; and follow after righteousness, godliness, faith, love, patience, meekness. Fight the good fight of faith, lay hold on eternal life, whereunto thou art also called, and hast professed a good profession before many witnesses. I give thee charge in the sight of God, who quickeneth all things, and before Christ Jesus, who before Pontius Pilate witnessed a good confession; that thou keep this commandment without spot, unrebukeable, until the appearing of our Lord Jesus Christ.   1 TIMOTHY 6:11–14

Take heed therefore unto yourselves, and to all the flock, over the which the Holy Ghost hath made you overseers, to feed the church of God, which he hath purchased with his own blood.   ACTS 20:28

Let the deacons be the husbands of one wife, ruling their children and their own houses well. For they that have used the office of a deacon well purchase to themselves a good degree, and great boldness in the faith which is in Christ Jesus.   1 TIMOTHY 3:12–13

Holding fast the faithful word as he hath been taught, that he may be able by sound doctrine both to exhort and to convince the gainsayers.   TITUS 1:9

Let no man despise thy youth; but be thou an example of the believers, in word, in conversation, in charity, in spirit, in faith, in purity.
1 TIMOTHY 4:12

A bishop then must be blameless, the husband of one wife, vigilant, sober, of good behaviour, given to hospitality, apt to teach; not given to wine, no striker, not greedy of filthy lucre; but patient, not a brawler, not covetous; one that ruleth well his own house, having his children in subjection with all gravity; (for if a man know not how to rule his own house, how shall he take care of the church of God?) not a novice, lest being lifted up with pride he fall into the condemnation of the devil. Moreover he must have a good report of them which are without; lest he fall into reproach and the snare of the devil.   1 TIMOTHY 3:2–7

Neglect not the gift that is in thee, which was given thee by prophecy.   1 TIMOTHY 4:14

Whosoever transgresseth, and abideth not in the doctrine of Christ, hath not God. He that abideth in the doctrine of Christ, he hath both the Father and the Son. If there come any unto you, and bring not this doctrine, receive him not into your house, neither bid him God speed: For he that biddeth him God speed is partaker of his evil deeds.   2 JOHN 9–11

Treat people as if they were

what they ought to be,

and you help them to become

what they are capable of being.

JOHANN WOLFGANG VON GOETHE

Now then we are ambassadors for Christ, as though God did beseech you by us: we pray you in Christ's stead, be ye reconciled to God.   2 CORINTHIANS 5:20

LOVE OF OTHERS

Brotherly love is still the
distinguishing badge of every true Christian.

Matthew Henry

And now abideth faith, hope, charity, these three; but the greatest of these is charity. 1 Corinthians 13:13

Ye have heard that it hath been said, Thou shalt love thy neighbour, and hate thine enemy. But I say unto you, Love your enemies, bless them that curse you, do good to them that hate you, and pray for them which despitefully use you, and persecute you; that ye may be the children of your Father which is in heaven: for he maketh his sun to rise on the evil and on the good, and sendeth rain on the just and on the unjust. Matthew 5:43–45

For this is the message that ye heard from the beginning, that we should love one another. 1 John 3:11

Thou shalt not avenge, nor bear any grudge against the children of thy people, but thou shalt love thy neighbour as thyself: I am the LORD.   LEVITICUS 19:18

Though I speak with the tongues of men and of angels, and have not charity, I am become as sounding brass, or a tinkling cymbal. And though I have the gift of prophecy, and understand all myster-ies, and all knowledge; and though I have all faith, so that I could remove mountains, and have not charity, I am nothing. And though I bestow all my goods to feed the poor, and though I give my body to be burned, and have not charity, it profiteth me nothing.
                                                          1 CORINTHIANS 13:1–3

"Love thy neighbor" is a precept which

could transform the world

if it were universally practiced.

MARY MCLEOD BETHUNE

If a man say, I love God, and hateth his brother, he is a liar: for he that loveth not his brother whom he hath seen, how can he love God whom he hath not seen? And this commandment have we from him, that he who loveth God love his brother also.   1 JOHN 4:20–21

In this the children of God are manifest, and the children of the devil: whosoever doeth not righteousness is not of God, neither he that loveth not his brother.   1 JOHN 3:10

Leave there thy gift before the altar, and go thy way; first be rec-onciled to thy brother, and then come and offer thy gift.
                                                          MATTHEW 5:24

This is my commandment, That ye love one another, as I have loved you. Greater love hath no man than this, that a man lay down his life for his friends.   JOHN 15:12–13

I speak to your shame. Is it so, that there is not a wise man among you? no, not one that shall be able to judge between his brethren? But brother goeth to law with brother, and that before the unbelievers. Now therefore there is utterly a fault among you, because ye go to law one with another. Why do ye not rather take wrong? why do ye not rather suffer yourselves to be defrauded? Nay, ye do wrong, and defraud, and that your brethren.   1 CORINTHIANS 6:5–8

Owe no man any thing, but to love one another: for he that loveth another hath fulfilled the law.   ROMANS 13:8

Be kindly affectioned one to another with brotherly love; in honour preferring one another.   ROMANS 12:10

And let us consider one another to provoke unto love and to good works.   HEBREWS 10:24

But as touching brotherly love ye need not that I write unto you: for ye yourselves are taught of God to love one another.
                                      1 THESSALONIANS 4:9

For all the law is fulfilled in one word, even in this; Thou shalt love thy neighbour as thyself.   GALATIANS 5:14

Beloved, if God so loved us, we ought also to love one another. No man hath seen God at any time. If we love one another, God dwelleth in us, and his love is perfected in us.   1 JOHN 4:11–12

Seeing ye have purified your souls in obeying the truth through the Spirit unto unfeigned love of the brethren, see that ye love one another with a pure heart fervently.   1 PETER 1:22

Honour all men. Love the brotherhood. Fear God. Honour the king.   1 PETER 2:17

Hereby perceive we the love of God, because he laid down his life for us: and we ought to lay down our lives for the brethren. But whoso hath this world's good, and seeth his brother have need, and shutteth up his bowels of compassion from him, how dwelleth the love of God in him? My little children, let us not love in word, neither in tongue; but in deed and in truth. And hereby we know that we are of the truth, and shall assure our hearts before him.   1 JOHN 3:16–19

And this I pray, that your love may abound yet more and more in knowledge and in all judgment.   PHILIPPIANS 1:9

And through thy knowledge shall the weak brother perish, for whom Christ died? But when ye sin so against the brethren, and wound their weak conscience, ye sin against Christ.   1 CORINTHIANS 8:11–12

A new commandment I give unto you, That ye love one another; as I have loved you, that ye also love one another. By this shall all men know that ye are my disciples, if ye have love one to another.
                                                          JOHN 13:34–35

My little children, let us not love in word, neither in tongue; but in deed and in truth.   1 JOHN 3:18

Beloved, let us loved one another: for love is of God; and every one that loveth is born of God, and knoweth God. He that loveth not knoweth not God; for God is love.   1 JOHN 4:7–8

Put on therefore, as the elect of God, holy and beloved, bowels of mercies, kindness, humbleness of mind, meekness, longsuffering; forbearing one another, and forgiving one another, if any man have a quarrel against any: even as Christ forgave you, so also do ye.
                                                          COLOSSIANS 3:12–13

LYING

Lie not, neither to thyself, nor man, nor God.
It is for cowards to lie.

GEORGE HERBERT

Lie not one to another, seeing that ye have put off the old man with his deeds; and have put on the new man, which is renewed in knowledge after the image of him that created him.

COLOSSIANS 3:9–10

And ye shall not swear by my name falsely, neither shalt thou profane the name of thy God: I am the LORD. LEVITICUS 19:12

A man that beareth false witness against his neighbour is a maul, and a sword, and a sharp arrow. PROVERBS 25:18

A faithful witness will not lie: but a false witness will utter lies.

PROVERBS 14:5

Thou shalt not raise a false report: put not thine hand with the wicked to be an unrighteous witness.   EXODUS 23:1

A false witness shall not be unpunished, and he that speaketh lies shall not escape.   PROVERBS 19:5

If a false witness rise up against any man to testify against him that which is wrong; then both the men, between whom the controversy is, shall stand before the LORD, before the priests and the judges, which shall be in those days; and the judges shall make diligent inquisition: and, behold, if the witness be a false witness, and hath testified falsely against his brother; then shall ye do unto him, as he had thought to have done unto his brother: so shalt thou put the evil away from among you.   DEUTERONOMY 19:16–19

A liar is not believed

even though he tell the truth.

MARCUS TULLIUS CICERO

A false witness shall not be unpunished, and he that speaketh lies shall perish.   PROVERBS 19:9

Be not a witness against thy neighbour without cause; and deceive not with thy lips.   PROVERBS 24:28

The wicked are estranged from the womb: they go astray as soon as they be born, speaking lies.   PSALM 58:3

But if ye have bitter envying and strife in your hearts, glory not, and lie not against the truth.   JAMES 3:14

The lip of truth shall be established for ever: but a lying tongue is but for a moment.   PROVERBS 12:19

But the fearful, and unbelieving, and the abominable, and murderers, and whoremongers, and sorcerers, and idolaters, and all liars, shall have their part in the lake which burneth with fire and brimstone: which is the second death.   REVELATION 21:8

Meekness

It is not the glorious battlements,
the painted windows,
the crouching gargoyles that support a building,
but the stones that lie unseen in or upon the earth.
It is often those who are despised and trampled on
that bear up the weight of a whole nation.

John Owen

Blessed are the meek: for they shall inherit the earth.

Matthew 5:5

But with righteousness shall he judge the poor, and reprove with equity for the meek of the earth.   Isaiah 11:4

The meek also shall increase their joy in the LORD, and the poor among men shall rejoice in the Holy One of Israel.   Isaiah 29:19

The LORD lifteth up the meek: he casteth the wicked down to the ground.
PSALM 147:6

The meek will he guide in judgment: and the meek will he teach his way.
PSALM 25:9

But the meek shall inherit the earth; and shall delight themselves in the abundance of peace.
PSALM 37:11

The humblest individual exerts some influence,

either for good or evil, upon others.

HENRY WARD BEECHER

A soft answer turneth away wrath: but grievous words stir up anger.
PROVERBS 15:1

Seek ye the LORD, all ye meek of the earth, which have wrought his judgment; seek righteousness, seek meekness: it may be ye shall be hid in the day of the LORD's anger.
ZEPHANIAH 2:3

But let it be the hidden man of the heart, in that which is not corruptible, even the ornament of a meek and quiet spirit, which is in the sight of God of great price.
1 PETER 3:4

The meek shall eat and be satisfied: they shall praise the LORD that seek him: your heart shall live for ever.
PSALM 22:26

For the LORD taketh pleasure in his people: he will beautify the meek with salvation.
PSALM 149:4

MERCY

Teach me to
feel another's woe,
To hide the fault I see;
That mercy I to others show,
That mercy show to me.

ALEXANDER POPE

Thou art a God ready to pardon, gracious and merciful, slow to anger, and of great kindness. NEHEMIAH 9:17

For God hath concluded them all in unbelief, that he might have mercy upon all. ROMANS 11:32

Let not mercy and truth forsake thee: bind them about thy neck; write them upon the table of thine heart: So shalt thou find favour and good understanding in the sight of God and man.

PROVERBS 3:3–4

He hath shewed thee, O man, what is good; and what doth the LORD require of thee, but to do justly, and to love mercy, and to walk humbly with thy God? MICAH 6:8

For thou, LORD, art good, and ready to forgive; and plenteous in mercy unto all them that call upon thee. PSALM 86:5

The LORD is good to all: and his tender mercies are over all his works. PSALM 145:9

Be ye therefore merciful, as your Father also is merciful. LUKE 6:36

And his mercy is on them that fear him from generation to generation. LUKE 1:50

Blessed are the merciful: for they shall obtain mercy. MATTHEW 5:7

Let the wicked forsake his way, and the unrighteous man his thoughts: and let him return unto the LORD, and he will have mercy upon him; and to our God, for he will abundantly pardon. ISAIAH 55:7

He that covereth his sins shall not prosper: but whoso confesseth and forsaketh them shall have mercy. PROVERBS 28:13

Mercy and truth are met together; righteousness and peace have kissed each other. PSALM 85:10

But thou, O LORD, art a God full of compassion, and gracious, longsuffering, and plenteous in mercy and truth. PSALM 86:15

Know therefore that God exacteth of thee less than thine iniquity deserveth. JOB 11:6

Not by works of righteousness which we have done, but according to his mercy he saved us, by the washing of regeneration, and renewing of the Holy Ghost; which he shed on us abundantly through Jesus Christ our Saviour; that being justified by his grace, we should be made heirs according to the hope of eternal life.　TITUS 3:5–7

For I will be merciful to their unrighteousness, and their sins and their iniquities will I remember no more. In that he saith, A new covenant, he hath made the first old. Now that which decayeth and waxeth old is ready to vanish away.　HEBREWS 8:12–13

And therefore will the LORD wait, that he may be gracious unto you, and therefore will he be exalted, that he may have mercy upon you: for the LORD is a God of judgment: blessed are all they that wait for him.　ISAIAH 30:18

Grace is when

God gives us what we don't deserve and

mercy is when

God doesn't give us what we do deserve.

DAN ROBERTS

And he said, I will make all my goodness pass before thee, and I will proclaim the name of the LORD before thee; and will be gracious to whom I will be gracious, and will shew mercy on whom I will shew mercy.　EXODUS 33:19

For in my wrath I smote thee, but in my favour have I had mercy on thee.　ISAIAH 60:10

And I will have mercy upon her that had not obtained mercy; and I will say to them which were not my people, Thou art my people; and they shall say, Thou art my God. HOSEA 2:23

For my name's sake will I defer mine anger, and for my praise will I refrain for thee, that I cut thee not off. ISAIAH 48:9

MONEY

*If a person gets
his attitude toward money straight,
it will help straighten out
almost every other area in his life.*

BILLY GRAHAM

For which of you, intending to build a tower, sitteth not down first, and counteth the cost, whether he have sufficient to finish it? Lest haply, after he hath laid the foundation, and is not able to finish it, all that behold it begin to mock him, Saying, This man began to build, and was not able to finish.   LUKE 14:28–30

A good man leaveth an inheritance to his children's children: and the wealth of the sinner is laid up for the just.   PROVERBS 13:22

He that loveth pleasure shall be a poor man: he that loveth wine and oil shall not be rich.   PROVERBS 21:17

And he saith unto them, Whose is this image and superscription? They say unto him, Caesar's. Then saith he unto them, Render therefore unto Caesar the things which are Caesar's; and unto God the things that are God's.   Matthew 22:20–21

The rich ruleth over the poor, and the borrower is servant to the lender.   Proverbs 22:7

Be not thou one of them that strike hands, or of them that are sureties for debts. If thou hast nothing to pay, why should he take away thy bed from under thee?   Proverbs 22:26–27

A little that a righteous man hath is better than the riches of many wicked.   Psalm 37:16

Hearken, my beloved brethren, Hath not God chosen the poor of this world rich in faith, and heirs of the kingdom which he hath promised to them that love him?   James 2:5

Whoso mocketh the poor reproacheth his Maker: and he that is glad at calamities shall not be unpunished.   Proverbs 17:5

He will regard the prayer of the destitute, and not despise their prayer.   Psalm 102:17

For the oppression of the poor, for the sighing of the needy, now will I arise, saith the Lord; I will set him in safety from him that puffeth at him.   Psalm 12:5

Better is little with the fear of the Lord than great treasure and trouble therewith.   Proverbs 15:16

For the needy shall not alway be forgotten: the expectation of the poor shall not perish for ever.   Psalm 9:18

Charge them that are rich in this world, that they be not high-minded, nor trust in uncertain riches, but in the living God, who giveth us richly all things to enjoy; that they do good, that they be rich in good works, ready to distribute, willing to communicate; laying up in store for themselves a good foundation against the time to come, that they may lay hold on eternal life.

1 TIMOTHY 6:17–19

Although I am poor, yet I fear my God,

and I will never take any money but such

as I can get in an honest manner.

Did God see fit, He could make me richer

in one day than I should become

were I for a long life to use every wicked means.

MARY MARTHA SHERWOOD

He that trusteth in his riches shall fall: but the righteous shall flourish as a branch.   PROVERBS 11:28

Riches profit not in the day of wrath: but righteousness delivereth from death.   PROVERBS 11:4

He that oppresseth the poor to increase his riches, and he that giveth to the rich, shall surely come to want.   PROVERBS 22:16

He that hasteth to be rich hath an evil eye, and considereth not that poverty shall come upon him.   PROVERBS 28:22

But thou shalt remember the LORD thy God: for it is he that giveth thee power to get wealth, that he may establish his covenant which he sware unto thy fathers, as it is this day.

DEUTERONOMY 8:18

He that loveth silver shall not be satisfied with silver; nor he that loveth abundance with increase: this is also vanity.

ECCLESIASTES 5:10

Blessed is he that considereth the poor: the LORD will deliver him in time of trouble.

PSALM 41:1

Yet setteth he the poor on high from affliction, and maketh him families like a flock.

PSALM 107:41

OBEDIENCE

Only he who believes is obedient.
Only he who is obedient, believes.

DIETRICH BONHOEFFER

My son, forget not my law; but let thine heart keep my commandments: for length of days, and long life, and peace, shall they add to thee.   PROVERBS 3:1–2

I command thee this day to love the LORD thy God, to walk in his ways, and to keep his commandments and his statutes and his judgments, that thou mayest live and multiply: and the LORD thy God shall bless thee in the land whither thou goest to possess it.   DEUTERONOMY 30:16

But whoso looketh into the perfect law of liberty, and continueth therein, he being not a forgetful hearer, but a doer of the work, this man shall be blessed in his deed.   JAMES 1:25

If they obey and serve him, they shall spend their days in prosperity, and their years in pleasures.   JOB 36:11

Let us hear the conclusion of the whole matter: Fear God, and keep his commandments: for this is the whole duty of man.

ECCLESIASTES 12:13

If ye keep my commandments, ye shall abide in my love; even as I have kept my Father's commandments, and abide in his love.

JOHN 15:10

And the world passeth away, and the lust thereof: but he that doeth the will of God abideth for ever.   1 JOHN 2:17

And Samuel said, Hath the Lord as great delight in burnt offerings and sacrifices, as in obeying the voice of the Lord? Behold, to obey is better than sacrifice, and to hearken than the fat of rams.

1 SAMUEL 15:22

Whosoever therefore shall break one of these least commandments, and shall teach men so, he shall be called the least in the kingdom of heaven: but whosoever shall do and teach them, the same shall be called great in the kingdom of heaven.   MATTHEW 5:19

For not the hearers of the law are just before God, but the doers of the law shall be justified.   ROMANS 2:13

Keep therefore the words of this covenant, and do them, that ye may prosper in all that ye do.   DEUTERONOMY 29:9

Hear therefore, O Israel, and observe to do it; that it may be well with thee, and that ye may increase mightily, as the LORD God of thy fathers hath promised thee, in the land that floweth with milk and honey.   DEUTERONOMY 6:3

Furthermore we have had fathers of our flesh which corrected us, and we gave them reverence: shall we not much rather be in subjection unto the Father of spirits, and live?   HEBREWS 12:9

But he said, Yea rather, blessed are they that hear the word of God, and keep it.   LUKE 11:28

And thou shalt do that which is right and good in the sight of the LORD.   DEUTERONOMY 6:18

No one can sum up all God is able to

accomplish through one solitary life,

wholly yielded, adjusted, and obedient to Him.

D. L. MOODY

Wherefore it shall come to pass, if ye hearken to these judgments, and keep, and do them, that the LORD thy God shall keep unto thee the covenant and the mercy which he sware unto thy fathers.
                                              DEUTERONOMY 7:12

O that there were such an heart in them, that they would fear me, and keep all my commandments always, that it might be well with them, and with their children for ever!   DEUTERONOMY 5:29

And we know that all things work together for good to them that love God, to them who are the called according to his purpose.
                                                  ROMANS 8:28

For whosoever shall do the will of my Father which is in heaven, the same is my brother, and sister, and mother.   MATTHEW 12:50

Therefore whosoever heareth these sayings of mine, and doeth them, I will liken him unto a wise man, which built his house upon a rock: And the rain descended, and the floods came, and the winds blew, and beat upon that house; and it fell not: for it was founded upon a rock.   MATTHEW 7:24–25

And whatsoever we ask, we receive of him, because we keep his commandments, and do those things that are pleasing in his sight.
                                                            1 JOHN 3:22

PATIENCE

*Our patience will
achieve more than
our force.*

EDMUND BURKE

For ye have need of patience, that, after ye have done the will of God, ye might receive the promise.   HEBREWS 10:36

Rest in the LORD, and wait patiently for him: fret not thyself because of him who prospereth in his way, because of the man who bringeth wicked devices to pass. Cease from anger, and forsake wrath: fret not thyself in any wise to do evil. For evildoers shall be cut off: but those that wait upon the LORD, they shall inherit the earth.
PSALM 37:7–9

And let us not be weary in well doing: for in due season we shall reap, if we faint not.   GALATIANS 6:9

Knowing this, that the trying of your faith worketh patience. But let patience have her perfect work, that ye may be perfect and entire, wanting nothing.   JAMES 1:3–4

But that on the good ground are they, which in an honest and good heart, having heard the word, keep it, and bring forth fruit with patience.   LUKE 8:15

And not only so, but we glory in tribulations also: knowing that tribulation worketh patience; and patience, experience; and experience, hope.   ROMANS 5:3–4

Here is the patience of the saints: here are they that keep the commandments of God, and the faith of Jesus.   REVELATION 14:12

But in all things approving ourselves as the ministers of God, in much patience, in afflictions, in necessities, in distresses.
                                    2 CORINTHIANS 6:4

For whatsoever things were written aforetime were written for our learning, that we through patience and comfort of the scriptures might have hope. Now the God of patience and consolation grant you to be likeminded one toward another according to Christ Jesus.
                                    ROMANS 15:4–5

Now we exhort you, brethren, warn them that are unruly, comfort the feebleminded, support the weak, be patient toward all men.
                                    1 THESSALONIANS 5:14

That ye be not slothful, but followers of them who through faith and patience inherit the promises.   HEBREWS 6:12

And the Lord direct your hearts into the love of God, and into the patient waiting for Christ.   2 THESSALONIANS 3:5

Be patient therefore, brethren, unto the coming of the Lord. Behold, the husbandman waiteth for the precious fruit of the earth, and hath long patience for it, until he receive the early and latter rain. Be ye also patient; stablish your hearts: for the coming of the Lord draweth nigh.   JAMES 5:7–8

Wherefore seeing we also are compassed about with so great a cloud of witnesses, let us lay aside every weight, and the sin which doth so easily beset us, and let us run with patience the race that is set before us.   HEBREWS 12:1

Be assured that,

if God waits longer than you could wish,

it is only to make the blessing doubly precious!

God waited four thousand years,

till the fullness of time, ere He sent His Son.

Our times are in His hands;

He will avenge His elect speedily;

He will make haste for our help

and not delay one hour too long.

ANDREW MURRAY

To them who by patient continuance in well doing seek for glory and honour and immortality, eternal life.   ROMANS 2:7

In your patience possess ye your souls.   LUKE 21:19

Better is the end of a thing than the beginning thereof: and the patient in spirit is better than the proud in spirit. Be not hasty in thy spirit to be angry: for anger resteth in the bosom of fools.

ECCLESIASTES 7:8–9

And so, after he had patiently endured, he obtained the promise.

HEBREWS 6:15

PEACE

Christ alone
can bring lasting peace—
peace with God—
peace among men and nations—
and peace within our hearts.

BILLY GRAHAM

Blessed are the peacemakers: for they shall be called the children of God. MATTHEW 5:9

And the fruit of righteousness is sown in peace of them that make peace. JAMES 3:18

Peace I leave with you, my peace I give unto you: not as the world giveth, give I unto you. Let not your heart be troubled, neither let it be afraid. JOHN 14:27

Endeavouring to keep the unity of the Spirit in the bond of peace.

EPHESIANS 4:3

Glory to God in the highest, and on earth peace, good will toward men.

LUKE 2:14

Mark the perfect man, and behold the upright: for the end of that man is peace.

PSALM 37:37

If it be possible, as much as lieth in you, live peaceably with all men.

ROMANS 12:18

And the peace of God, which passeth all understanding, shall keep your hearts and minds through Christ Jesus.

PHILIPPIANS 4:7

Behold, how good and how pleasant it is for brethren to dwell together in unity!

PSALM 133:1

I exhort therefore, that, first of all, supplications, prayers, intercessions, and giving of thanks, be made for all men; for kings, and for all that are in authority; that we may lead a quiet and peaceable life in all godliness and honesty.

1 TIMOTHY 2:1–2

For God hath not given us the spirit of fear; but of power, and of love, and of a sound mind.

2 TIMOTHY 1:7

For he that will love life, and see good days, let him refrain his tongue from evil, and his lips that they speak no guile: Let him eschew evil, and do good; let him seek peace, and ensue it.

1 PETER 3:10–11

Thou wilt keep him in perfect peace, whose mind is stayed on thee: because he trusteth in thee.

ISAIAH 26:3

Let the peace of God rule in your hearts.

COLOSSIANS 3:15

Peace, peace to him that is far off, and to him that is near, saith the LORD; and I will heal him.   ISAIAH 57:19

I will hear what God the LORD will speak: for he will speak peace unto his people, and to his saints.   PSALM 85:8

When peace, like a river, attendeth my way,

When sorrows like sea billows roll;

Whatever my lot, Thou has thought me to say,

"It is well, it is well, with my soul."

HORATIO G. SPAFFORD

And the work of righteousness shall be peace; and the effect of righteousness quietness and assurance for ever.   ISAIAH 32:17

Thy faith hath saved thee; go in peace.   LUKE 7:50

Now the Lord of peace himself give you peace always by all means.
2 THESSALONIANS 3:16

PERSEVERANCE

Nothing in this world
can take the place of persistence.
Talent will not;
nothing is more common
than unsuccessful men with talent.
Genius will not;
unrewarded genius is almost a proverb.
Education will not;
the world is full of educated derelicts.
Persistence and determination alone
are omnipotent.

CALVIN COOLIDGE

Let us hold fast the profession of our faith without wavering; (for he is faithful that promised). HEBREWS 10:23

But the path of the just is as the shining light, that shineth more and more unto the perfect day.   PROVERBS 4:18

To him that overcometh will I grant to sit with me in my throne, even as I also overcame, and am set down with my Father in his throne.   REVELATION 3:21

Then said Jesus to those Jews which believed on him, If ye continue in my word, then are ye my disciples indeed.   JOHN 8:31

In the confrontation between

the stream and the rock,

the stream always wins—

not through strength but by perseverance.

H. JACKSON BROWN

Ye therefore, beloved, seeing ye know these things before, beware lest ye also, being led away with the error of the wicked, fall from your own stedfastness.   2 PETER 3:17

Confirming the souls of the disciples, and exhorting them to continue in the faith, and that we must through much tribulation enter into the kingdom of God.   ACTS 14:22

Who shall separate us from the love of Christ? shall tribulation, or distress, or persecution, or famine, or nakedness, or peril, or sword?   ROMANS 8:35

For now we live, if ye stand fast in the Lord.   1 THESSALONIANS 3:8

Wherefore take unto you the whole armour of God, that ye may be able to withstand in the evil day, and having done all, to stand.

EPHESIANS 6:13

Though he fall, he shall not be utterly cast down: for the LORD upholdeth him with his hand. PSALM 37:24

Wherefore seeing we also are compassed about with so great a cloud of witnesses, let us lay aside every weight, and the sin which doth so easily beset us, and let us run with patience the race that is set before us, looking unto Jesus the author and finisher of our faith; who for the joy that was set before him endured the cross, despising the shame, and is set down at the right hand of the throne of God. HEBREWS 12:1–2

Therefore, my brethren dearly beloved and longed for, my joy and crown, so stand fast in the Lord, my dearly beloved.

PHILIPPIANS 4:1

For the which cause I also suffer these things: nevertheless I am not ashamed: for I know whom I have believed, and am persuaded that he is able to keep that which I have committed unto him against that day. Hold fast the form of sound words, which thou hast heard of me, in faith and love which is in Christ Jesus.

2 TIMOTHY 1:12–13

He that hath an ear, let him hear what the Spirit saith unto the churches; He that overcometh shall not be hurt of the second death. REVELATION 2:11

That the trial of your faith, being much more precious than of gold that perisheth, though it be tried with fire, might be found unto praise and honour and glory at the appearing of Jesus Christ.

1 PETER 1:7

For we are made partakers of Christ, if we hold the beginning of
our confidence stedfast unto the end.   HEBREWS 3:14

Praying always with all prayer and supplication in the Spirit, and
watching thereunto with all perseverance and supplication for all
saints.   EPHESIANS 6:18

POWER

*An infinite God can
give all of Himself to
each of His children.
He does not distribute Himself
that each may have a part,
but to each one He gives
all of Himself as fully as if
there were no others.*

A. W. TOZER

Now unto him that is able to do exceeding abundantly above all
that we ask or think, according to the power that worketh in us.

EPHESIANS 3:20

Seek the Lord and his strength, seek his face continually.

1 CHRONICLES 16:11

But ye shall receive power, after that the Holy Ghost is come upon you: and ye shall be witnesses unto me both in Jerusalem, and in all Judaea, and in Samaria, and unto the uttermost part of the earth.   ACTS 1:8

Consider, my soul,

the mightiness of the Lord

who is thy glory and defence.

He is a man of war;

Jehovah is His name.

All the forces of heaven are at His beck,

legions wait at His door,

cherubim and seraphim;

watchers and holy ones,

principalities and powers,

are all attentive to His will.

CHARLES H. SPURGEON

And what is the exceeding greatness of his power to us-ward who believe, according to the working of his mighty power, which he wrought in Christ, when he raised him from the dead, and set him at his own right hand in the heavenly places.   EPHESIANS 1:19–20

For our gospel came not unto you in word only, but also in power, and in the Holy Ghost, and in much assurance; as ye know what manner of men we were among you for your sake.

1 THESSALONIANS 1:5

For the kingdom of God is not in word, but in power.

1 CORINTHIANS 4:20

The LORD thy God in the midst of thee is mighty; he will save, he will rejoice over thee with joy; he will rest in his love, he will joy over thee with singing. ZEPHANIAH 3:17

And have tasted the good word of God, and the powers of the world to come. HEBREWS 6:5

PRAYER

Fear not because your prayer is stammering,
your words feeble, and your language poor.
Jesus can understand you.
Just as a mother understands
the first lispings of her infant,
so does the blessed Savior understand sinners.
He can read a sigh and see a meaning in a groan.

J. C. RYLE

But thou, when thou prayest, enter into thy closet, and when thou hast shut thy door, pray to thy Father which is in secret; and thy Father which seeth in secret shall reward thee openly. But when ye pray, use not vain repetitions, as the heathen do: for they think that they shall be heard for their much speaking. Be not ye therefore like unto them: for your Father knoweth what things ye have need of, before ye ask him. MATTHEW 6:6–8

But we will give ourselves continually to prayer, and to the ministry of the word.   ACTS 6:4

Likewise the Spirit also helpeth our infirmities: for we know not what we should pray for as we ought: but the Spirit itself maketh intercession for us with groanings which cannot be uttered.

ROMANS 8:26

Give ear to my words, O LORD, consider my meditation. Hearken unto the voice of my cry, my King, and my God: for unto thee will I pray. My voice shalt thou hear in the morning, O LORD; in the morning will I direct my prayer unto thee, and will look up.

PSALM 5:1–3

He will be very gracious unto thee at the voice of thy cry; when he shall hear it, he will answer thee.   ISAIAH 30:19

I waited patiently for the LORD; and he inclined unto me, and heard my cry.   PSALM 40:1

And shall not God avenge his own elect, which cry day and night unto him, though he bear long with them?   LUKE 18:7

And all things, whatsoever ye shall ask in prayer, believing, ye shall receive.   MATTHEW 21:22

Because he hath inclined his ear unto me, therefore will I call upon him as long as I live.   PSALM 116:2

Let us therefore come boldly unto the throne of grace, that we may obtain mercy, and find grace to help in time of need.

HEBREWS 4:16

Then shall ye call upon me, and ye shall go and pray unto me, and I will hearken unto you.   JEREMIAH 29:12

If my people, which are called by my name, shall humble them-selves, and pray, and seek my face, and turn from their wicked ways; then will I hear from heaven, and will forgive their sin, and will heal their land.   2 CHRONICLES 7:14

Ask, and it shall be given you; seek, and ye shall find; knock, and it shall be opened unto you: For every one that asketh receiveth; and he that seeketh findeth; and to him that knocketh it shall be opened.   MATTHEW 7:7–8

God speaks to me

not through the thunder and the earthquake,

nor through the ocean and the stars,

but through the Son of Man,

and speaks in a language adapted to

my imperfect sight and hearing.

WILLIAM LYON PHELPS

Confess your faults one to another, and pray one for another, that ye may be healed. The effectual fervent prayer of a righteous man availeth much.   JAMES 5:16

Yet the LORD will command his lovingkindness in the daytime, and in the night his song shall be with me, and my prayer unto the God of my life.   PSALM 42:8

Pray without ceasing.   1 THESSALONIANS 5:17

And this is the confidence that we have in him, that, if we ask any thing according to his will, he heareth us: And if we know that he hear us, whatsoever we ask, we know that we have the petitions that we desired of him.   1 JOHN 5:14–15

In prayer it is better to have

a heart without words

than words without a heart.

JOHN BUNYAN

And it shall come to pass, that before they call, I will answer; and while they are yet speaking, I will hear.   ISAIAH 65:24

The righteous cry, and the LORD heareth, and delivereth them out of all their troubles.   PSALM 34:17

The LORD is nigh unto all them that call upon him, to all that call upon him in truth. He will fulfil the desire of them that fear him: he also will hear their cry, and will save them.   PSALM 145:18–19

Rejoicing in hope; patient in tribulation; continuing instant in prayer.   ROMANS 12:12

Evening, and morning, and at noon, will I pray, and cry aloud: and he shall hear my voice.   PSALM 55:17

PRIDE

There is one vice of which no man in the world is free;
which everyone in the world loathes
when he sees it in someone else;
and of which hardly any people, except Christians
ever imagine that they are guilty themselves. . . .
The essential vice, the utmost evil, is Pride.
Unchastity, anger, greed, drunkenness, and all that,
are mere fleabites in comparison:
it was through Pride that the devil became the devil;
Pride leads to every other vice:
It is the complete anti-God state of mind. . . .
As long as you are proud you cannot know God.
A proud man is always looking down on things and people;
and, of course, as long as you are looking down,
you cannot see something that is above you.

C. S. LEWIS

And he sat down, and called the twelve, and saith unto them, If any man desire to be first, the same shall be last of all, and servant of all.   MARK 9:35

Surely God will not hear vanity, neither will the Almighty regard it.
                                                          JOB 35:13

An high look, and a proud heart, and the plowing of the wicked, is sin.   PROVERBS 21:4

But now ye rejoice in your boastings: all such rejoicing is evil.
                                                          JAMES 4:16

Be of the same mind one toward another. Mind not high things, but condescend to men of low estate. Be not wise in your own conceits.
                                                          ROMANS 12:16

Which receive honour one of another, and seek not the honour that cometh from God only?   JOHN 5:44

Woe unto them that are wise in their own eyes, and prudent in their own sight!   ISAIAH 5:21

Talk no more so exceeding proudly; let not arrogancy come out of your mouth: for the Lord is a God of knowledge, and by him actions are weighed.   1 SAMUEL 2:3

The fear of the LORD is to hate evil: pride, and arrogancy, and the evil way, and the froward mouth, do I hate.   PROVERBS 8:13

Pride goeth before destruction, and an haughty spirit before a fall.
                                                          PROVERBS 16:18

Let not the foot of pride come against me, and let not the hand of the wicked remove me.   PSALM 36:11

And he said unto them, Ye are they which justify yourselves before men; but God knoweth your hearts: for that which is highly esteemed among men is abomination in the sight of God.

LUKE 16:15

He that is of a proud heart stirreth up strife: but he that putteth his trust in the LORD shall be made fat. He that trusteth in his own heart is a fool: but whoso walketh wisely, he shall be delivered.

PROVERBS 28:25–26

I believe firmly that the moment our hearts

are emptied of pride and selfishness

and ambition and everything that is

contrary to God's law,

the Holy Spirit will fill every corner of our hearts.

But if we are full of pride and conceit

and ambition and the world,

there is no room for the Spirit of God.

D. L. MOODY

When pride cometh, then cometh shame: but with the lowly is wisdom.   PROVERBS 11:2

For if a man think himself to be something, when he is nothing, he deceiveth himself.   GALATIANS 6:3

For I say, through the grace given unto me, to every man that is among you, not to think of himself more highly than he ought to think; but to think soberly, according as God hath dealt to every man the measure of faith.   ROMANS 12:3

But he that glorieth, let him glory in the Lord. For not he that commendeth himself is approved, but whom the Lord commendeth.
                                        2 CORINTHIANS 10:17–18

Seest thou a man wise in his own conceit? there is more hope of a fool than of him.   PROVERBS 26:12

Let another man praise thee, and not thine own mouth; a stranger, and not thine own lips.   PROVERBS 27:2

Thou hast rebuked the proud that are cursed, which do err from thy commandments.   PSALM 119:21

PURITY/LUST

No one can make himself pure by obeying laws.
Jesus Christ does not give us rules and regulations—
He gives us His teachings which are truths
that can only be interpreted by His nature
which He places within us.

OSWALD CHAMBERS

Who can find a virtuous woman? for her price is far above rubies.
PROVERBS 31:10

Thou shalt not commit adultery.   EXODUS 20:14

Ye have heard that it was said by them of old time, Thou shalt not commit adultery: But I say unto you, That whosoever looketh on a woman to lust after her hath committed adultery with her already in his heart.   MATTHEW 5:27–28

To keep thee from the evil woman, from the flattery of the tongue of a strange woman. Lust not after her beauty in thine heart; neither let her take thee with her eyelids. For by means of a whorish woman a man is brought to a piece of bread: and the adulteress will hunt for the precious life. Can a man take fire in his bosom, and his clothes not be burned? Can one go upon hot coals, and his feet not be burned? So he that goeth in to his neighbour's wife; whosoever toucheth her shall not be innocent. PROVERBS 6:24–29

For this is the will of God, even your sanctification, that ye should abstain from fornication. 1 THESSALONIANS 4:3

Mortify therefore your members which are upon the earth; fornication, uncleanness, inordinate affection, evil concupiscence, and covetousness, which is idolatry: For which things' sake the wrath of God cometh on the children of disobedience. COLOSSIANS 3:5–6

I made a covenant with mine eyes; why then should I think upon a maid? JOB 31:1

Meats for the belly, and the belly for meats: but God shall destroy both it and them. Now the body is not for fornication, but for the Lord; and the Lord for the body. And God hath both raised up the Lord, and will also raise up us by his own power. Know ye not that your bodies are the members of Christ? shall I then take the members of Christ, and make them the members of an harlot? God forbid. What? know ye not that he which is joined to an harlot is one body? for two, saith he, shall be one flesh. But he that is joined unto the Lord is one spirit. Flee fornication. Every sin that a man doeth is without the body; but he that committeth fornication sinneth against his own body. What? know ye not that your body is the temple of the Holy Ghost which is in you, which ye have of God, and ye are not your own? For ye are bought with a price: therefore glorify God in your body, and in your spirit, which are God's. 1 CORINTHIANS 6:13–20

There hath no temptation taken you but such as is common to man: but God is faithful, who will not suffer you to be tempted above that ye are able; but will with the temptation also make a way to escape, that ye may be able to bear it.   1 CORINTHIANS 10:13

Blessed is the man that endureth temptation: for when he is tried, he shall receive the crown of life, which the Lord hath promised to them that love him.   JAMES 1:12

Lord, cleanse my mind of things

I've seen, heard, and read that have filled my mind

with confused, idle thoughts.

Remove what I've let build up bit by bit.

Help me refocus on only what is

pure, lovely, and right in Your eyes.

REBECCA GERMANY

For all that is in the world, the lust of the flesh, and the lust of the eyes, and the pride of life, is not of the Father, but is of the world. And the world passeth away, and the lust thereof: but he that doeth the will of God abideth for ever.   1 JOHN 2:16–17

Dearly beloved, I beseech you as strangers and pilgrims, abstain from fleshly lusts, which war against the soul.   1 PETER 2:11

Marriage is honourable in all, and the bed undefiled: but whoremongers and adulterers God will judge.   HEBREWS 13:4

From whence come wars and fightings among you? come they not hence, even of your lusts that war in your members? Ye lust, and have not: ye kill, and desire to have, and cannot obtain: ye fight and war, yet ye have not, because ye ask not. Ye ask, and receive not, because ye ask amiss, that ye may consume it upon your lusts. Ye adulterers and adulteresses, know ye not that the friendship of the world is enmity with God? whosoever therefore will be a friend of the world is the enemy of God.   JAMES 4:1–4

Submit yourselves therefore to God. Resist the devil, and he will flee from you. Draw nigh to God, and he will draw nigh to you. Cleanse your hands, ye sinners; and purify your hearts, ye double minded.   JAMES 4:7–8

As obedient children, not fashioning yourselves according to the former lusts in your ignorance: But as he which hath called you is holy, so be ye holy in all manner of conversation; because it is written, Be ye holy; for I am holy.   1 PETER 1:14–16

And they that are Christ's have crucified the flesh with the affections and lusts.   GALATIANS 5:24

Flee also youthful lusts: but follow righteousness, faith, charity, peace, with them that call on the Lord out of a pure heart.

2 TIMOTHY 2:22

Now concerning the things whereof ye wrote unto me: It is good for a man not to touch a woman.   1 CORINTHIANS 7:1

They told you there should be mockers in the last time, who should walk after their own ungodly lusts. These be they who separate themselves, sensual, having not the Spirit. But ye, beloved, building up yourselves on your most holy faith, praying in the Holy Ghost, keep yourselves in the love of God, looking for the mercy of our Lord Jesus Christ unto eternal life.   JUDE 18–21

For we ourselves also were sometimes foolish, disobedient, deceived, serving divers lusts and pleasures, living in malice and envy, hateful, and hating one another. But after that the kindness and love of God our Saviour toward man appeared, not by works of righteousness which we have done, but according to his mercy he saved us, by the washing of regeneration, and renewing of the Holy Ghost.

TITUS 3:3–5

God would not rub so hard if it were not

to fetch out the dirt that is ingrained in our natures.

God loves purity so well

He had rather see a hole

than a spot in His child's garments.

WILLIAM GURNALL

We all had our conversation in times past in the lusts of our flesh, fulfilling the desires of the flesh and of the mind; and were by nature the children of wrath, even as others. But God, who is rich in mercy, for his great love wherewith he loved us, even when we were dead in sins, hath quickened us together with Christ, (by grace ye are saved;) and hath raised us up together, and made us sit together in heavenly places in Christ Jesus.   EPHESIANS 2:3–6

Likewise reckon ye also yourselves to be dead indeed unto sin, but alive unto God through Jesus Christ our Lord. Let not sin therefore reign in your mortal body, that ye should obey it in the lusts thereof. For sin shall not have dominion over you: for ye are not under the law, but under grace.   ROMANS 6:11–12, 14

I say therefore to the unmarried and widows, it is good for them if they abide even as I. But if they cannot contain, let them marry: for it is better to marry than to burn. 1 CORINTHIANS 7:8–9

For the grace of God that bringeth salvation hath appeared to all men, teaching us that, denying ungodliness and worldly lusts, we should live soberly, righteously, and godly, in this present world. TITUS 2:11–12

Walk in the Spirit, and ye shall not fulfil the lust of the flesh. For the flesh lusteth against the Spirit, and the Spirit against the flesh: and these are contrary the one to the other: so that ye cannot do the things that ye would. GALATIANS 5:16–17

But put ye on the Lord Jesus Christ, and make not provision for the flesh, to fulfil the lusts thereof. ROMANS 13:14

REPENTANCE

*Repentance is
a change of willing,
of feeling, and of living,
in respect to God.*

CHARLES FINNEY

Repent ye therefore, and be converted, that your sins may be blotted out, when the times of refreshing shall come from the presence of the Lord.   ACTS 3:19

I will have mercy, and not sacrifice: for I am not come to call the righteous, but sinners to repentance.   MATTHEW 9:13

He looketh upon men, and if any say, I have sinned, and perverted that which was right, and it profited me not; He will deliver his soul from going into the pit, and his life shall see the light.
JOB 33:27–28

Likewise, I say unto you, there is joy in the presence of the angels of God over one sinner that repenteth.   LUKE 15:10

The time is fulfilled, and the kingdom of God is at hand: repent ye, and believe the gospel.   MARK 1:15

Remember therefore how thou hast received and heard, and hold fast, and repent. If therefore thou shalt not watch, I will come on thee as a thief, and thou shalt not know what hour I will come upon thee.   REVELATION 3:3

He that covereth his sins shall not prosper: but whoso confesseth and forsaketh them shall have mercy.   PROVERBS 28:13

Or despisest thou the riches of his goodness and forbearance and longsuffering; not knowing that the goodness of God leadeth thee to repentance?   ROMANS 2:4

Turn unto the LORD your God: for he is gracious and merciful, slow to anger, and of great kindness, and repenteth him of the evil.   JOEL 2:13

Seek ye the LORD while he may be found, call ye upon him while he is near: Let the wicked forsake his way, and the unrighteous man his thoughts: and let him return unto the LORD, and he will have mercy upon him; and to our God, for he will abundantly pardon.   ISAIAH 55:6–7

And saying, The time is fulfilled, and the kingdom of God is at hand: repent ye, and believe the gospel.   MARK 1:15

The LORD is nigh unto them that are of a broken heart; and saveth such as be of a contrite spirit.   PSALM 34:18

He healeth the broken in heart, and bindeth up their wounds.   PSALM 147:3

If iniquity be in thine hand, put it far away, and let not wickedness dwell in thy tabernacles. For then shalt thou lift up thy face without spot; yea, thou shalt be stedfast, and shalt not fear.

JOB 11:14–15

True repentance will entirely change you;

the bias of your souls will be changed,

then you will delight in God, in Christ,

in His Law, and in His people.

GEORGE WHITEFIELD

But if the wicked will turn from all his sins that he hath committed, and keep all my statutes, and do that which is lawful and right, he shall surely live, he shall not die. All his transgressions that he hath committed, they shall not be mentioned unto him: in his righteousness that he hath done he shall live.   EZEKIEL 18:21–22

REPUTATION

A cross Christian, or an anxious Christian,
a discouraged, gloomy Christian,
a doubting Christian, a complaining Christian,
an exacting Christian,
a selfish Christian, a cruel, hard-hearted Christian,
a self-indulgent Christian,
a Christian with a sharp tongue or bitter spirit,
all these may be very earnest in their work
and may have honorable places in the church;
but they are not Christlike Christians.

HANNAH WHITALL SMITH

Every man's work shall be made manifest: for the day shall declare it, because it shall be revealed by fire; and the fire shall try every man's work of what sort it is.   1 CORINTHIANS 3:13

Neither do men light a candle, and put it under a bushel, but on a candlestick; and it giveth light unto all that are in the house. Let your light so shine before men, that they may see your good works, and glorify your Father which is in heaven.   MATTHEW 5:15–16

A good name is rather to be chosen than great riches, and loving favour rather than silver and gold.   PROVERBS 22:1

But he that doeth truth cometh to the light, that his deeds may be made manifest, that they are wrought in God.   JOHN 3:21

If I take care of my character,

my reputation will take care of me.

D. L. MOODY

Ye shall know them by their fruits. Do men gather grapes of thorns, or figs of thistles? Even so every good tree bringeth forth good fruit; but a corrupt tree bringeth forth evil fruit. A good tree cannot bring forth evil fruit, neither can a corrupt tree bring forth good fruit. Every tree that bringeth not forth good fruit is hewn down, and cast into the fire. Wherefore by their fruits ye shall know them.
    MATTHEW 7:16–20

Now therefore ye are no more strangers and foreigners, but fellow-citizens with the saints, and of the household of God; and are built upon the foundation of the apostles and prophets, Jesus Christ himself being the chief corner stone.   EPHESIANS 2:19–20

A good name is better than precious ointment; and the day of death than the day of one's birth.   ECCLESIASTES 7:1

Only let your conversation be as it becometh the gospel of Christ: that whether I come and see you, or else be absent, I may hear of your affairs, that ye stand fast in one spirit, with one mind striving together for the faith of the gospel; and in nothing terrified by your adversaries: which is to them an evident token of perdition, but to you of salvation, and that of God.   PHILIPPIANS 1:27–28

Therefore, seeing we have this ministry, as we have received mercy, we faint not; but have renounced the hidden things of dishonesty, not walking in craftiness, nor handling the word of God deceitfully; but by manifestation of the truth commending ourselves to every man's conscience in the sight of God.   2 CORINTHIANS 4:1–2

Blessed is the man that walketh not in the counsel of the ungodly, nor standeth in the way of sinners, nor sitteth in the seat of the scornful.   PSALM 1:1

RESPONSIBILITY

The most important thought
that ever occupied my mind is that of
my individual responsibility to God.

DANIEL WEBSTER

Now he that planteth and he that watereth are one: and every man shall receive his own reward according to his own labour.

1 CORINTHIANS 3:8

The soul that sinneth, it shall die. The son shall not bear the iniquity of the father, neither shall the father bear the iniquity of the son: the righteousness of the righteous shall be upon him, and the wickedness of the wicked shall be upon him.   EZEKIEL 18:20

For by thy words thou shalt be justified, and by thy words thou shalt be condemned.   MATTHEW 12:37

I am he which searcheth the reins and hearts: and I will give unto every one of you according to your works.   REVELATION 2:23

And he said, Now also let it be according unto your words: he with whom it is found shall be my servant; and ye shall be blameless.

GENESIS 44:10

That ye may be blameless and harmless, the sons of God, without rebuke, in the midst of a crooked and perverse nation, among whom ye shine as lights in the world.   PHILIPPIANS 2:15

It is the duty of every Christian

to be Christ to his neighbor.

MARTIN LUTHER

Dearly beloved, I beseech you as strangers and pilgrims, abstain from fleshly lusts, which war against the soul; having your conversation honest among the Gentiles: that, whereas they speak against you as evildoers, they may by your good works, which they shall behold, glorify God in the day of visitation. Submit yourselves to every ordinance of man for the Lord's sake: whether it be to the king, as supreme; or unto governors, as unto them that are sent by him for the punishment of evildoers, and for the praise of them that do well. For so is the will of God, that with well doing ye may put to silence the ignorance of foolish men: as free, and not using your liberty for a cloke of maliciousness, but as the servants of God.   1 PETER 2:11–16

And they were both righteous before God, walking in all the commandments and ordinances of the Lord blameless.   LUKE 1:6

For every man shall bear his own burden.   GALATIANS 6:5

Therefore I will judge you, O house of Israel, every one according to his ways, saith the Lord GOD. Repent, and turn yourselves from all your transgressions; so iniquity shall not be your ruin.
                                                  EZEKIEL 18:30

Rest

Every now and then go away,
have a little relaxation,
for when you come back
to your work your judgment
will be surer.

Leonardo da Vinci

And thou shalt be secure, because there is hope; yea, thou shalt dig about thee, and thou shalt take thy rest in safety.　　Job 11:18

When thou liest down, thou shalt not be afraid: yea, thou shalt lie down, and thy sleep shall be sweet.　　Proverbs 3:24

For he spake in a certain place of the seventh day on this wise, and God did rest the seventh day from all his works. . . . There remaineth therefore a rest to the people of God.　　Hebrews 4:4, 9

Six days may work be done; but in the seventh is the sabbath of rest, holy to the LORD. EXODUS 31:15

It is vain for you to rise up early, to sit up late, to eat the bread of sorrows: for so he giveth his beloved sleep. PSALM 127:2

Now the day is over,

Night is drawing nigh,

Shadows of the evening

Steal across the sky.

Jesus, give the weary

Calm and sweet repose;

With Thy tend'rest blessing

May our eyelids close.

When the morning wakens

Then may I arise

Pure and fresh and sinless

In Thy holy eyes.

SABINE BARING-GOULD

He that dwelleth in the secret place of the most High shall abide under the shadow of the Almighty. PSALM 91:1

RIGHTEOUSNESS

The man of life upright,
Whose guiltless heart is free
From all dishonest deeds
Or thought of vanity.

THOMAS CAMPION

Then shall the righteous shine forth as the sun in the kingdom of their Father. Who hath ears to hear, let him hear.

MATTHEW 13:43

The righteous cry, and the LORD heareth, and delivereth them out of all their troubles.

PSALM 34:17

But if thou shalt indeed obey his voice, and do all that I speak; then I will be an enemy unto thine enemies, and an adversary unto thine adversaries.

EXODUS 23:22

The eyes of the LORD are upon the righteous, and his ears are open unto their cry.   PSALM 34:15

If we confess our sins, he is faithful and just to forgive us our sins, and to cleanse us from all unrighteousness.   1 JOHN 1:9

God is not looking for brilliant men,

is not depending upon eloquent men,

is not shut up to the use of talented men

in sending His gospel out in the world.

God is looking for broken men

who have judged themselves in

the light of the cross of Christ.

When He wants anything done,

He takes up men who have

come to the end of themselves,

whose confidence is not in themselves, but in God.

H. A. IRONSIDE

Ye that love the LORD, hate evil: he preserveth the souls of his saints; he delivereth them out of the hand of the wicked. Light is sown for the righteous.   PSALM 97:10–11

And it shall come to pass, if thou shalt hearken diligently unto the voice of the LORD thy God, to observe and to do all his commandments which I command thee this day, that the LORD thy God will set thee on high above all nations of the earth.

DEUTERONOMY 28:1

He withdraweth not his eyes from the righteous: but with kings are they on the throne; yea, he doth establish them for ever, and they are exalted.

JOB 36:7

The LORD will not suffer the soul of the righteous to famish: but he casteth away the substance of the wicked.

PROVERBS 10:3

Then shall thy light break forth as the morning, and thine health shall spring forth speedily: and thy righteousness shall go before thee; the glory of the LORD shall be thy reward.

ISAIAH 58:8

He that followeth after righteousness and mercy findeth life, righteousness, and honour.

PROVERBS 21:21

The righteous shall be glad in the LORD, and shall trust in him; and all the upright in heart shall glory.

PSALM 64:10

Blessed are they which do hunger and thirst after righteousness: for they shall be filled.

MATTHEW 5:6

A righteous man hateth lying: but a wicked man is loathsome, and cometh to shame.

PROVERBS 13:5

Blessed are they which are persecuted for righteousness' sake: for theirs is the kingdom of heaven.

MATTHEW 5:10

LORD, who shall abide in thy tabernacle? who shall dwell in thy holy hill? He that walketh uprightly, and worketh righteousness, and speaketh the truth in his heart.

PSALM 15:1–2

Know ye not that the unrighteous shall not inherit the kingdom of God? Be not deceived.   1 CORINTHIANS 6:9

Then shall he answer them, saying, Verily I say unto you, Inasmuch as ye did it not to one of the least of these, ye did it not to me. And these shall go away into everlasting punishment: but the righteous into life eternal.   MATTHEW 25:45–46

For the LORD God is a sun and shield: the LORD will give grace and glory: no good thing will he withhold from them that walk uprightly.   PSALM 84:11

The fear of the wicked, it shall come upon him: but the desire of the righteous shall be granted.   PROVERBS 10:24

Evil pursueth sinners: but to the righteous good shall be repayed.
                                                  PROVERBS 13:21

But seek ye first the kingdom of God, and his righteousness; and all these things shall be added unto you.   MATTHEW 6:33

So that a man shall say, Verily there is a reward for the righteous.
                                                   PSALM 58:11

For thou, LORD, wilt bless the righteous; with favour wilt thou compass him as with a shield.   PSALM 5:12

Say ye to the righteous, that it shall be well with him: for they shall eat the fruit of their doings.   ISAIAH 3:10

SALVATION

Give your life to God;
he can do more with it than you can!

D. L. MOODY

Jesus answered and said unto him, Verily, verily, I say unto thee, Except a man be born again, he cannot see the kingdom of God. Nicodemus saith unto him, How can a man be born when he is old? can he enter the second time into his mother's womb, and be born? Jesus answered, Verily, verily, I say unto thee, Except a man be born of water and of the Spirit, he cannot enter into the kingdom of God. That which is born of the flesh is flesh; and that which is born of the Spirit is spirit. Marvel not that I said unto thee, Ye must be born again. JOHN 3:3–7

Neither is there salvation in any other: for there is none other name under heaven given among men, whereby we must be saved.

ACTS 4:12

He that believeth on the Son hath everlasting life.   JOHN 3:36

My little children, these things write I unto you, that ye sin not. And if any man sin, we have an advocate with the Father, Jesus Christ the righteous: and he is the propitiation for our sins: and not for ours only, but also for the sins of the whole world.   1 JOHN 2:1–2

But as many as received him, to them gave he power to become the sons of God, even to them that believe on his name: which were born, not of blood, nor of the will of the flesh, nor of the will of man, but of God.   JOHN 1:12–13

Christ is the desire of nations,

the joy of angels,

the delight of the Father.

What solace then must

that soul be filled with,

that has the possession

of Him to all eternity!

JOHN BUNYAN

But after that the kindness and love of God our Saviour toward man appeared, not by works of righteousness which we have done, but according to his mercy he saved us, by the washing of regeneration, and renewing of the Holy Ghost; which he shed on us abundantly through Jesus Christ our Saviour.   TITUS 3:4–6

For he hath made him to be sin for us, who knew no sin; that we might be made the righteousness of God in him.

2 Corinthians 5:21

Even as I please all men in all things, not seeking mine own profit, but the profit of many, that they may be saved.

1 Corinthians 10:33

Therefore if any man be in Christ, he is a new creature: old things are passed away; behold, all things are become new.

2 Corinthians 5:17

For this is good and acceptable in the sight of God our Saviour; who will have all men to be saved, and to come unto the knowledge of the truth.   1 Timothy 2:3–4

And you, being dead in your sins and the uncircumcision of your flesh, hath he quickened together with him, having forgiven you all trespasses.   Colossians 2:13

But not as the offence, so also is the free gift. For if through the offence of one many be dead, much more the grace of God, and the gift by grace, which is by one man, Jesus Christ, hath abounded unto many.   Romans 5:15

The Lord is with you, while ye be with him; and if ye seek him, he will be found of you; but if ye forsake him, he will forsake you.

2 Chronicles 15:2

And they that know thy name will put their trust in thee: for thou, Lord, hast not forsaken them that seek thee.   Psalm 9:10

And ye shall seek me, and find me, when ye shall search for me with all your heart.   Jeremiah 29:13

Seek the LORD, and ye shall live.   AMOS 5:6

For I am not ashamed of the gospel of Christ: for it is the power of God unto salvation to every one that believeth.   ROMANS 1:16

SCRIPTURE

We are to believe and follow Christ in all things,
including His words about scripture.
And this means that scripture is
to be for us what it was to Him:
the unique, authoritative, and inerrant Word of God,
and not merely a human testimony to Christ,
however carefully guided and preserved by God.
If the Bible is less than this to us,
we are not fully Christ's disciples.

JAMES MONTGOMERY BOICE

God, who at sundry times and in divers manners spake in time past unto the fathers by the prophets, hath in these last days spoken unto us by his Son, whom he hath appointed heir of all things, by whom also he made the worlds.   HEBREWS 1:1–2

So shall my word be that goeth forth out of my mouth: it shall not return unto me void, but it shall accomplish that which I please, and it shall prosper in the thing whereto I sent it.   ISAIAH 55:11

This book of the law shall not depart out of thy mouth; but thou shalt meditate therein day and night, that thou mayest observe to do according to all that is written therein: for then thou shalt make thy way prosperous, and then thou shalt have good success.

JOSHUA 1:8

The Bible is a book of faith,

and a book of doctrine,

and a book of morals,

and a book of religion,

of especial revelation from God.

DANIEL WEBSTER

That ye may be mindful of the words which were spoken before by the holy prophets, and of the commandment of us the apostles of the Lord and Saviour.   2 PETER 3:2

Thy word have I hid in mine heart, that I might not sin against thee.   PSALM 119:11

Let the word of Christ dwell in you richly in all wisdom; teaching and admonishing one another in psalms and hymns and spiritual songs, singing with grace in your hearts to the Lord.

COLOSSIANS 3:16

Blessed is he that readeth, and they that hear the words of this prophecy, and keep those things which are written therein: for the time is at hand.   REVELATION 1:3

Thy word is a lamp unto my feet, and a light unto my path.

PSALM 119:105

Therefore shall ye lay up these my words in your heart and in your soul, and bind them for a sign upon your hand, that they may be as frontlets between your eyes. And ye shall teach them your children, speaking of them when thou sittest in thine house, and when thou walkest by the way, when thou liest down, and when thou risest up.   DEUTERONOMY 11:18–19

For the word of God is quick, and powerful, and sharper than any twoedged sword, piercing even to the dividing asunder of soul and spirit, and of the joints and marrow, and is a discerner of the thoughts and intents of the heart.   HEBREWS 4:12

We have also a more sure word of prophecy; whereunto ye do well that ye take heed, as unto a light that shineth in a dark place, until the day dawn, and the day star arise in your hearts.   2 PETER 1:19

Search the scriptures; for in them ye think ye have eternal life: and they are they which testify of me.   JOHN 5:39

For the commandment is a lamp; and the law is light; and reproofs of instruction are the way of life.   PROVERBS 6:23

The entrance of thy words giveth light; it giveth understanding unto the simple.   PSALM 119:130

And now, brethren, I commend you to God, and to the word of his grace, which is able to build you up, and to give you an inheritance among all them which are sanctified.   ACTS 20:32

And that from a child thou hast known the holy scriptures, which are able to make thee wise unto salvation through faith which is in Christ Jesus. All scripture is given by inspiration of God, and is profitable for doctrine, for reproof, for correction, for instruction in righteousness. 2 TIMOTHY 3:15–16

So then faith cometh by hearing, and hearing by the word of God. ROMANS 10:17

Wherefore lay apart all filthiness and superfluity of naughtiness, and receive with meekness the engrafted word, which is able to save your souls. But be ye doers of the word, and not hearers only, deceiving your own selves. For if any be a hearer of the word, and not a doer, he is like unto a man beholding his natural face in a glass: For he beholdeth himself, and goeth his way, and straightway forgetteth what manner of man he was. But whoso looketh into the perfect law of liberty, and continueth therein, he being not a forgetful hearer, but a doer of the work, this man shall be blessed in his deed. JAMES 1:21–25

Being born again, not of corruptible seed, but of incorruptible, by the word of God, which liveth and abideth for ever. 1 PETER 1:23

As newborn babes, desire the sincere milk of the word, that ye may grow thereby. 1 PETER 2:2

SELF-CONTROL

He who reigns within himself
and rules passions, desires, and fears
is more than a king.

JOHN MILTON

Then said Pilate unto him, Hearest thou not how many things they witness against thee? And he answered him to never a word; insomuch that the governor marvelled greatly.   MATTHEW 27:13–14

If the spirit of the ruler rise up against thee, leave not thy place; for yielding pacifieth great offences.   ECCLESIASTES 10:4

For even hereunto were ye called: because Christ also suffered for us, leaving us an example, that ye should follow his steps: who did no sin, neither was guile found in his mouth: who, when he was reviled, reviled not again; when he suffered, he threatened not; but committed himself to him that judgeth righteously.   1 PETER 2:21–23

Charity suffereth long, and is kind; charity envieth not; charity vaunteth not itself, is not puffed up, doth not behave itself unseemly, seeketh not her own, is not easily provoked, thinketh no evil.

1 CORINTHIANS 13:4–5

Yet Michael the archangel, when contending with the devil he disputed about the body of Moses, durst not bring against him a railing accusation, but said, The Lord rebuke thee.   JUDE 9

Let us walk honestly, as in the day; not in rioting and drunkenness, not in chambering and wantonness, not in strife and envying. But put ye on the Lord Jesus Christ, and make not provision for the flesh, to fulfil the lusts thereof.   ROMANS 13:13–14

Hast thou found honey? eat so much as is sufficient for thee, lest thou be filled therewith, and vomit it.   PROVERBS 25:16

Let your moderation be known unto all men. The Lord is at hand.

PHILIPPIANS 4:5

Therefore let us not sleep, as do others; but let us watch and be sober. For they that sleep sleep in the night; and they that be drunken are drunken in the night.   1 THESSALONIANS 5:6–7

And beside this, giving all diligence, add to your faith virtue; and to virtue knowledge; and to knowledge temperance; and to temperance patience; and to patience godliness.   2 PETER 1:5–6

And every man that striveth for the mastery is temperate in all things. Now they do it to obtain a corruptible crown; but we an incorruptible.   1 CORINTHIANS 9:25

But I keep under my body, and bring it into subjection: lest that by any means, when I have preached to others, I myself should be a castaway.   1 CORINTHIANS 9:27

For if ye live after the flesh, ye shall die: but if ye through the Spirit do mortify the deeds of the body, ye shall live.   ROMANS 8:13

Teaching us that, denying ungodliness and worldly lusts, we should live soberly, righteously, and godly, in this present world.

         TITUS 2:12

He sitteth alone and keepeth silence, because he hath borne it upon him. He putteth his mouth in the dust; if so be there may be hope.   LAMENTATIONS 3:28–29

Out of one hundred men,

one will read the Bible;

the other ninety-nine will read the Christian.

D. L. MOODY

Be grave, not doubletongued, not given to much wine, not greedy of filthy lucre.   1 TIMOTHY 3:8

Neither fornicators, nor idolaters, nor adulterers, nor effeminate, nor abusers of themselves with mankind, nor thieves, nor covetous, nor drunkards, nor revilers, nor extortioners, shall inherit the kingdom of God. And such were some of you: but ye are washed, but ye are sanctified, but ye are justified in the name of the Lord Jesus, and by the Spirit of our God.   1 CORINTHIANS 6:9–11

SICKNESS

Is any sick among you?
let him call for the elders of the church;
and let them pray over him,
anointing him with oil in the name of the Lord:
And the prayer of faith shall save the sick,
and the Lord shall raise him up;
and if he have committed sins,
they shall be forgiven him.
Confess your faults one to another,
and pray one for another, that ye may be healed.
The effectual fervent prayer
of a righteous man availeth much.

JAMES 5:14–16

And when he was come into the house, the blind men came to him: and Jesus saith unto them, Believe ye that I am able to do this? They said unto him, Yea, Lord. Then touched he their eyes, saying, According to your faith be it unto you. And their eyes were opened.   MATTHEW 9:28–30

But that ye may know that the Son of man hath power on earth to forgive sins, (then saith he to the sick of the palsy,) Arise, take up thy bed, and go unto thine house. And he arose, and departed to his house.   MATTHEW 9:6–7

And Jesus went about all Galilee, teaching in their synagogues, and preaching the gospel of the kingdom, and healing all manner of sickness and all manner of disease among the people. And his fame went throughout all Syria: and they brought unto him all sick people that were taken with divers diseases and torments, and those which were possessed with devils, and those which were lunatic, and those that had the palsy; and he healed them.   MATTHEW 4:23–24

For I will restore health unto thee, and I will heal thee of thy wounds, saith the LORD.   JEREMIAH 30:17

And ye shall serve the LORD your God, and he shall bless thy bread, and thy water; and I will take sickness away from the midst of thee.   EXODUS 23:25

SIN

If I had the wisdom of Solomon,
the patience of John,
the meekness of Moses,
the strength of Samson,
the obedience of Abraham,
the compassion of Joseph,
the tears of Jeremiah,
the poetic skill of David,
the prophetic voice of Elijah,
the courage of Daniel,
the greatness of John the Baptist,
the endurance and love of Paul,
I would still need redemption
through Christ's blood, the forgiveness of sin.

R. L. WHEELER

This is a faithful saying, and worthy of all acceptation, that Christ
Jesus came into the world to save sinners; of whom I am chief.

1 TIMOTHY 1:15

Come now, and let us reason together, saith the LORD: though
your sins be as scarlet, they shall be as white as snow; though they
be red like crimson, they shall be as wool.   ISAIAH 1:18

For this is my blood of the new testament, which is shed for many
for the remission of sins.   MATTHEW 26:28

Whatever weakens your reason,

impairs the tenderness of your conscience,

obscures your sense of God,

or takes off the relish for spiritual things,

then it is sin for you,

however innocent it may be in itself.

SUSANNA WESLEY

And she shall bring forth a son, and thou shalt call his name JESUS:
for he shall save his people from their sins.   MATTHEW 1:21

My little children, these things write I unto you, that ye sin not.
And if any man sin, we have an advocate with the Father, Jesus
Christ the righteous: And he is the propitiation for our sins: and
not for ours only, but also for the sins of the whole world.

1 JOHN 2:1–2

Therefore if any man be in Christ, he is a new creature: old things are passed away; behold, all things are become new.

2 CORINTHIANS 5:17

To him give all the prophets witness, that through his name whosoever believeth in him shall receive remission of sins.   ACTS 10:43

Who gave himself for our sins, that he might deliver us from this present evil world, according to the will of God and our Father.

GALATIANS 1:4

But he was wounded for our transgressions, he was bruised for our iniquities: the chastisement of our peace was upon him; and with his stripes we are healed. All we like sheep have gone astray; we have turned every one to his own way; and the LORD hath laid on him the iniquity of us all.   ISAIAH 53:5–6

Knowing this, that our old man is crucified with him, that the body of sin might be destroyed, that henceforth we should not serve sin. For he that is dead is freed from sin.   ROMANS 6:6–7

For I will be merciful to their unrighteousness, and their sins and their iniquities will I remember no more.   HEBREWS 8:12

For sin shall not have dominion over you: for ye are not under the law, but under grace.   ROMANS 6:14

The next day John seeth Jesus coming unto him, and saith, Behold the Lamb of God, which taketh away the sin of the world.

JOHN 1:29

Likewise reckon ye also yourselves to be dead indeed unto sin, but alive unto God through Jesus Christ our Lord.   ROMANS 6:11

Be it known unto you therefore, men and brethren, that through this man is preached unto you the forgiveness of sins.   ACTS 13:38

What shall we say then? Shall we continue in sin, that grace may abound? God forbid. How shall we, that are dead to sin, live any longer therein?

ROMANS 6:1–2

Then will I sprinkle clean water upon you, and ye shall be clean: from all your filthiness, and from all your idols, will I cleanse you. A new heart also will I give you, and a new spirit will I put within you: and I will take away the stony heart out of your flesh, and I will give you an heart of flesh.

EZEKIEL 36:25–26

It is impossible for a man to be freed from

the habit of sin before he hates it,

just as it is impossible to receive forgiveness

before confessing his trespasses.

IGNATIUS

In whom we have redemption through his blood, the forgiveness of sins, according to the riches of his grace.

EPHESIANS 1:7

And ye know that he was manifested to take away our sins; and in him is no sin.

1 JOHN 3:5

So Christ was once offered to bear the sins of many; and unto them that look for him shall he appear the second time without sin unto salvation.

HEBREWS 9:28

SINCERITY

Sincerity makes the very least person
to be of more value than
the most talented hypocrite.

CHARLES H. SPURGEON

As newborn babes, desire the sincere milk of the word, that ye may grow thereby.   1 PETER 2:2

For we are not as many, which corrupt the word of God: but as of sincerity, but as of God, in the sight of God speak we in Christ.
2 CORINTHIANS 2:17

Now therefore fear the LORD, and serve him in sincerity and in truth.   JOSHUA 24:14

Now the end of the commandment is charity out of a pure heart, and of a good conscience, and of faith unfeigned.   1 TIMOTHY 1:5

Seeing ye have purified your souls in obeying the truth through the Spirit unto unfeigned love of the brethren, see that ye love one another with a pure heart fervently. 1 PETER 1:22

My God, I give You this day.

I offer You, now,

all of the good that I shall do

and I promise to accept,

for love of You,

all of the difficulty that I shall meet.

Help me to conduct myself

during this day

in a manner pleasing to You.

Amen.

ST. FRANCIS DE SALES

What will ye do in the solemn day, and in the day of the feast of the LORD? HOSEA 9:5

For our rejoicing is this, the testimony of our conscience, that in simplicity and godly sincerity, not with fleshly wisdom, but by the grace of God, we have had our conversation in the world, and more abundantly to you-ward. 2 CORINTHIANS 1:12

Therefore let us keep the feast, not with old leaven, neither with the leaven of malice and wickedness; but with the unleavened bread of sincerity and truth.   1 CORINTHIANS 5:8

Grace be with all them that love our Lord Jesus Christ in sincerity. Amen.   EPHESIANS 6:24

Young men likewise exhort to be sober minded.   TITUS 2:6

For our exhortation was not of deceit, nor of uncleanness, nor in guile: But as we were allowed of God to be put in trust with the gospel, even so we speak; not as pleasing men, but God, which trieth our hearts. For neither at any time used we flattering words, as ye know, nor a cloke of covetousness; God is witness.
                                        1 THESSALONIANS 2:3–5

Wherefore laying aside all malice, and all guile, and hypocrisies, and envies, and all evil speakings.   1 PETER 2:1

That ye may approve things that are excellent; that ye may be sincere and without offence till the day of Christ.   PHILIPPIANS 1:10

I speak not by commandment, but by occasion of the forwardness of others, and to prove the sincerity of your love.
                                        2 CORINTHIANS 8:8

Blessed is the man unto whom the LORD imputeth not iniquity, and in whose spirit there is no guile.   PSALM 32:2

And in their mouth was found no guile: for they are without fault before the throne of God.   REVELATION 14:5

Wherefore gird up the loins of your mind, be sober, and hope to the end for the grace that is to be brought unto you at the revelation of Jesus Christ.   1 PETER 1:13

Let love be without dissimulation. Abhor that which is evil; cleave
to that which is good.   ROMANS 12:9

But let us, who are of the day, be sober, putting on the breastplate
of faith and love; and for an helmet, the hope of salvation.

1 THESSALONIANS 5:8

For I say, through the grace given unto me, to every man that is
among you, not to think of himself more highly than he ought to
think; but to think soberly, according as God hath dealt to every
man the measure of faith.   ROMANS 12:3

SLANDER AND REPROACH

Truth is generally the best
vindication against slander.

ABRAHAM LINCOLN

Thou shalt hide them in the secret of thy presence from the pride of man: thou shalt keep them secretly in a pavilion from the strife of tongues. PSALM 31:20

Thou shalt be hid from the scourge of the tongue: neither shalt thou be afraid of destruction when it cometh. JOB 5:21

I said, I will take heed to my ways, that I sin not with my tongue: I will keep my mouth with a bridle, while the wicked is before me. PSALM 39:1

In the multitude of words there wanteth not sin: but he that refraineth his lips is wise.   PROVERBS 10:19

These are the things that ye shall do; Speak ye every man the truth to his neighbour; execute the judgment of truth and peace in your gates.   ZECHARIAH 8:16

Set a watch, O LORD, before my mouth; keep the door of my lips.   PSALM 141:3

Slander cannot destroy an honest man—

when the flood recedes the rock is there.

CHINESE PROVERB

Blessed are ye, when men shall revile you, and persecute you, and shall say all manner of evil against you falsely, for my sake. Rejoice, and be exceeding glad: for great is your reward in heaven: for so persecuted they the prophets which were before you.   MATTHEW 5:11–12

If ye be reproached for the name of Christ, happy are ye; for the spirit of glory and of God resteth upon you: on their part he is evil spoken of, but on your part he is glorified.   1 PETER 4:14

He shall send from heaven, and save me from the reproach of him that would swallow me up. Selah. God shall send forth his mercy and his truth.   PSALM 57:3

Hearken unto me, ye that know righteousness, the people in whose heart is my law; fear ye not the reproach of men, neither be ye afraid of their revilings.   ISAIAH 51:7

But now ye also put off all these; anger, wrath, malice, blasphemy, filthy communication out of your mouth.   COLOSSIANS 3:8

And he shall bring forth thy righteousness as the light, and thy judgment as the noonday.   PSALM 37:6

And when they bring you unto the synagogues, and unto magistrates, and powers, take ye no thought how or what thing ye shall answer, or what ye shall say: For the Holy Ghost shall teach you in the same hour what ye ought to say.   LUKE 12:11–12

SOBRIETY

*Drinking was
a sin first,
and disease later.*

BILLY GRAHAM

Drunkenness, revellings, and such like: of the which I tell you before, as I have also told you in time past, that they which do such things shall not inherit the kingdom of God.   GALATIANS 5:21

Woe unto them that rise up early in the morning, that they may follow strong drink; that continue until night, till wine inflame them!   ISAIAH 5:11

For he shall be great in the sight of the Lord, and shall drink neither wine nor strong drink; and he shall be filled with the Holy Ghost, even from his mother's womb.   LUKE 1:15

Now therefore beware, I pray thee, and drink not wine nor strong drink, and eat not any unclean thing.   JUDGES 13:4

Wine is a mocker, strong drink is raging: and whosoever is deceived thereby is not wise.   PROVERBS 20:1

Who hath woe? who hath sorrow? who hath contentions? who hath babbling? who hath wounds without cause? who hath redness of eyes? They that tarry long at the wine; they that go to seek mixed wine. Look not thou upon the wine when it is red, when it giveth his colour in the cup, when it moveth itself aright. At the last it biteth like a serpent, and stingeth like an adder.   PROVERBS 23:29–32

Drinking makes such fools of people,

and people are such fools to begin with,

it's just compounding the felony.

ROBERT BENCHLEY

Woe unto him that giveth his neighbour drink, that puttest thy bottle to him, and makest him drunken also, that thou mayest look on their nakedness!   HABAKKUK 2:15

And take heed to yourselves, lest at any time your hearts be overcharged with surfeiting, and drunkenness, and cares of this life, and so that day come upon you unawares.   LUKE 21:34

For while they be folden together as thorns, and while they are drunken as drunkards, they shall be devoured as stubble fully dry.   NAHUM 1:10

And they have cast lots for my people; and have given a boy for an harlot, and sold a girl for wine, that they might drink.   JOEL 3:3

Whoredom and wine and new wine take away the heart.

HOSEA 4:11

For the drunkard and the glutton shall come to poverty: and drowsiness shall clothe a man with rags.   PROVERBS 23:21

STRENGTH

Do not pray for easy lives. Pray to be stronger men!
Do not pray for tasks equal to your powers.
Pray for power equal to your tasks.

PHILLIPS BROOKS

He giveth power to the faint; and to them that have no might he increaseth strength.   ISAIAH 40:29

Wait on the LORD: be of good courage, and he shall strengthen thine heart: wait, I say, on the LORD.   PSALM 27:14

The LORD will give strength unto his people; the LORD will bless his people with peace.   PSALM 29:11

For the eyes of the LORD run to and fro throughout the whole earth, to shew himself strong in the behalf of them whose heart is perfect toward him.   2 CHRONICLES 16:9

But they that wait upon the LORD shall renew their strength; they shall mount up with wings as eagles; they shall run, and not be weary; and they shall walk, and not faint.   ISAIAH 40:31

The LORD is my rock, and my fortress, and my deliverer; my God, my strength, in whom I will trust; my buckler, and the horn of my salvation, and my high tower.   PSALM 18:2

Have courage for the great sorrows of life

and patience for the small ones.

And when you have laboriously accomplished

your daily task, go to sleep in peace.

God is awake.

VICTOR HUGO

I know both how to be abased, and I know how to abound: every where and in all things I am instructed both to be full and to be hungry, both to abound and to suffer need. I can do all things through Christ which strengtheneth me.   PHILIPPIANS 4:12–13

By pureness, by knowledge, by longsuffering, by kindness, by the Holy Ghost, by love unfeigned, by the word of truth, by the power of God, by the armour of righteousness on the right hand and on the left.   2 CORINTHIANS 6:6–7

Both riches and honour come of thee, and thou reignest over all; and in thine hand is power and might; and in thine hand it is to make great, and to give strength unto all.   1 CHRONICLES 29:12

The righteous also shall hold on his way, and he that hath clean hands shall be stronger and stronger.   JOB 17:9

My flesh and my heart faileth: but God is the strength of my heart, and my portion for ever.   PSALM 73:26

That ye might walk worthy of the Lord unto all pleasing, being fruitful in every good work, and increasing in the knowledge of God; strengthened with all might, according to his glorious power, unto all patience and longsuffering with joyfulness.

COLOSSIANS 1:10–11

O God, thou art terrible out of thy holy places: the God of Israel is he that giveth strength and power unto his people. Blessed be God.   PSALM 68:35

And he said unto me, My grace is sufficient for thee: for my strength is made perfect in weakness. Most gladly therefore will I rather glory in my infirmities, that the power of Christ may rest upon me.   2 CORINTHIANS 12:9

Finally, my brethren, be strong in the Lord, and in the power of his might.   EPHESIANS 6:10

Nay, in all these things we are more than conquerors through him that loved us.   ROMANS 8:37

SUCCESS

We find in life exactly what we put into it.

RALPH WALDO EMERSON

In the house of the righteous is much treasure: but in the revenues of the wicked is trouble. PROVERBS 15:6

By humility and the fear of the LORD are riches, and honour, and life. PROVERBS 22:4

And the LORD thy God will make thee plenteous in every work of thine hand, in the fruit of thy body, and in the fruit of thy cattle, and in the fruit of thy land, for good: for the LORD will again rejoice over thee for good, as he rejoiced over thy fathers.

DEUTERONOMY 30:9

And also that every man should eat and drink, and enjoy the good of all his labour, it is the gift of God. ECCLESIASTES 3:13

And the LORD shall make thee plenteous in goods, in the fruit of thy body, and in the fruit of thy cattle, and in the fruit of thy ground, in the land which the LORD sware unto thy fathers to give thee. The LORD shall open unto thee his good treasure, the heaven to give the rain unto thy land in his season, and to bless all the work of thine hand: and thou shalt lend unto many nations, and thou shalt not borrow. And the LORD shall make thee the head, and not the tail; and thou shalt be above only, and thou shalt not beneath; if that thou hearken unto the commandments of the LORD thy God, which I command thee this day, to observe and to do them.   DEUTERONOMY 28:11–13·

Every man also to whom God hath given riches and wealth, and hath given him power to eat thereof, and to take his portion, and to rejoice in his labour; this is the gift of God.   ECCLESIASTES 5:19

Then shall he give the rain of thy seed, that thou shalt sow the ground withal; and bread of the increase of the earth, and it shall be fat and plenteous: in that day shall thy cattle feed in large pastures.
ISAIAH 30:23

And he shall be like a tree planted by the rivers of water, that bringeth forth his fruit in his season; his leaf also shall not wither; and whatsoever he doeth shall prosper.   PSALM 1:3

Riches and honour are with me; yea, durable riches and righteousness. My fruit is better than gold, yea, than fine gold; and my revenue than choice silver.   PROVERBS 8:18–19

Wealth and riches shall be in his house: and his righteousness endureth for ever.   PSALM 112:3

And I will send grass in thy fields for thy cattle, that thou mayest eat and be full.   DEUTERONOMY 11:15

Then shalt thou lay up gold as dust, and the gold of Ophir as the stones of the brooks. Yea, the Almighty shall be thy defence, and thou shalt have plenty of silver.

JOB 22:24–25

Thou shalt also decree a thing, and it shall be established unto thee: and the light shall shine upon thy ways.

JOB 22:28

For thou shalt eat the labour of thine hands: happy shalt thou be, and it shall be well with thee.

PSALM 128:2

Look at a day when you are

supremely satisfied at the end.

It is not a day when

you lounge around doing nothing;

it is when you have had everything to do,

and you have done it.

MARGARET THATCHER

For God hath not given us the spirit of fear; but of power, and of love, and of a sound mind.

2 TIMOTHY 1:7

Because the LORD thy God shall bless thee in all thine increase, and in all the works of thine hands, therefore thou shalt surely rejoice.

DEUTERONOMY 16:15

Be ye strong therefore, and let not your hands be weak: for your work shall be rewarded.

2 CHRONICLES 15:7

And they shall build houses, and inhabit them; and they shall plant vineyards, and eat the fruit of them. They shall not build, and another inhabit; they shall not plant, and another eat: for as the days of a tree are the days of my people, and mine elect shall long enjoy the work of their hands. They shall not labor in vain, nor bring forth for trouble; for they are the seed of the blessed of the LORD, and their offspring with them.   ISAIAH 65:21–23

And all these blessings shall come on thee, and overtake thee, if thou shalt hearken unto the voice of the LORD thy God. Blessed shalt thou be in the city, and blessed shalt thou be in the field. Blessed shall be the fruit of thy body, and the fruit of thy ground, and the fruit of thy cattle, the increase of thy kine, and the flocks of thy sheep. Blessed shall be thy basket and thy store. Blessed shalt thou be when thou comest in, and blessed shalt thou be when thou goest out.   DEUTERONOMY 28:2–6

Better is the end of a thing than the beginning thereof: and the patient in spirit is better than the proud in spirit.   ECCLESIASTES 7:8

Commit thy works unto the LORD, and thy thoughts shall be established.   PROVERBS 16:3

This book of the law shall not depart out of thy mouth; but thou shalt meditate therein day and night, that thou mayest observe to do according to all that is written therein: for then thou shalt make thy way prosperous, and then thou shalt have good success.
                    JOSHUA 1:8

TEMPTATION

*The reason why many fail in battle is
because they wait until the hour of battle.
The reason why others succeed is
because they have gained their victory
on their knees long before the battle came. . . .
Anticipate your battles;
fight them on your knees before temptation comes,
and you will always have victory.*

R. A. TORREY

Then was Jesus led up of the Spirit into the wilderness to be tempted of the devil.
MATTHEW 4:1

But they that will be rich fall into temptation and a snare, and into many foolish and hurtful lusts, which drown men in destruction and perdition.
1 TIMOTHY 6:9

And he was there in the wilderness forty days, tempted of Satan; and was with the wild beasts; and the angels ministered unto him.
MARK 1:13

Watch and pray, that ye enter not into temptation: the spirit indeed is willing, but the flesh is weak.   MATTHEW 26:41

And when he was at the place, he said unto them, Pray that ye enter not into temptation.   LUKE 22:40

And said unto them, Why sleep ye? rise and pray, lest ye enter into temptation.   LUKE 22:46

Neither let us tempt Christ, as some of them also tempted, and were destroyed of serpents.   1 CORINTHIANS 10:9

There hath no temptation taken you but such as is common to man: but God is faithful, who will not suffer you to be tempted above that ye are able; but will with the temptation also make a way to escape, that ye may be able to bear it.   1 CORINTHIANS 10:13

For in that he himself hath suffered being tempted, he is able to succour them that are tempted.   HEBREWS 2:18

And lead us not into temptation, but deliver us from evil: For thine is the kingdom, and the power, and the glory, for ever. Amen.
MATTHEW 6:13

Blessed is the man that endureth temptation: for when he is tried, he shall receive the crown of life, which the Lord hath promised to them that love him.   JAMES 1:12

Because thou hast kept the word of my patience, I also will keep thee from the hour of temptation, which shall come upon all the world, to try them that dwell upon the earth.   REVELATION 3:10

And when the devil had ended all the temptation, he departed from him for a season.

LUKE 4:13

Let no man say when he is tempted, I am tempted of God: for God cannot be tempted with evil, neither tempteth he any man.

JAMES 1:13

Watch constantly against those things

which are thought to be no temptations.

The most poisonous serpents are found

where the sweetest flowers grow.

Cleopatra was poisoned by an asp

that was brought to her in a basket of fair flowers.

Sharp-edged tools, long handled, wound at last.

CHARLES H. SPURGEON

The Lord knoweth how to deliver the godly out of temptations.

2 PETER 2:9

They on the rock are they, which, when they hear, receive the word with joy; and these have no root, which for a while believe, and in time of temptation fall away.

LUKE 8:13

Brethren, if a man be overtaken in a fault, ye which are spiritual, restore such an one in the spirit of meekness; considering thyself, lest thou also be tempted.

GALATIANS 6:1

My brethren, count it all joy when ye fall into divers temptations; Knowing this, that the trying of your faith worketh patience. But let patience have her perfect work, that ye may be perfect and entire, wanting nothing.   JAMES 1:2–4

TRUST

*To be trusted is a greater complement
than to be loved.*

GEORGE MACDONALD

God is our refuge and strength, a very present help in trouble. Therefore will not we fear, though the earth be removed, and though the
mountains be carried into the midst of the sea.　　PSALM 46:1–2

For the LORD God is a sun and shield: the LORD will give grace
and glory: no good thing will he withhold from them that walk
uprightly. O LORD of hosts, blessed is the man that trusteth in
thee.　　PSALM 84:11–12

Therefore take no thought, saying, What shall we eat? or, What shall
we drink? or, Wherewithal shall we be clothed? (For after all these
things do the Gentiles seek:) for your heavenly Father knoweth that
ye have need of all these things.　　MATTHEW 6:31–32

Trust in the LORD, and do good; so shalt thou dwell in the land, and verily thou shalt be fed. Delight thyself also in the LORD; and he shall give thee the desires of thine heart. Commit thy way unto the LORD; trust also in him; and he shall bring it to pass.

PSALM 37:3–5

Trust in the LORD with all thine heart; and lean not unto thine own understanding. In all thy ways acknowledge him, and he shall direct thy paths.   PROVERBS 3:5–6

Fear not, little flock; for it is your Father's good pleasure to give you the kingdom.   LUKE 12:32

In God, we live every commonplace

as well as the most exalted moment of our being.

To trust in Him when no need is pressing,

when things seem going right of themselves,

may be harder than when things seem going wrong.

GEORGE MACDONALD

Casting all your care upon him; for he careth for you.   1 PETER 5:7

They that trust in the LORD shall be as mount Zion, which cannot be removed, but abideth for ever.   PSALM 125:1

Blessed is that man that maketh the LORD his trust.   PSALM 40:4

TRUTH

*How can we know that what
Jesus has shown us of God is the truth;
or how do we know when we look into the face of Jesus
that we are looking into the face of God?
The answer is so plain and simple that it is a marvel
how intelligent men can manage to miss it as they do.
Look at what Christ has done for the soul of man:
That is your answer.
Christianity is just Christ—
nothing more and nothing less.
It is a way of life, and He is that way.
It is the truth about human destiny,
and He is that truth.*

R. J. CAMPBELL

Jesus saith unto him, I am the way, the truth, and the life: no man cometh unto the Father, but by me.   JOHN 14:6

He is the Rock, his work is perfect: for all his ways are judgment: a God of truth and without iniquity, just and right is he.
                                                    DEUTERONOMY 32:4

That he who blesseth himself in the earth shall bless himself in the God of truth; and he that sweareth in the earth shall swear by the God of truth.   ISAIAH 65:16

Finally, brethren, whatsoever things are true, whatsoever things are honest, whatsoever things are just, whatsoever things are pure, whatsoever things are lovely, whatsoever things are of good report; if there be any virtue, and if there be any praise, think on these things.   PHILIPPIANS 4:8

For the word of the LORD is right; and all his works are done in truth.   PSALM 33:4

And for their sakes I sanctify myself, that they also might be sanctified through the truth.   JOHN 17:19

These are the things that ye shall do; Speak ye every man the truth to his neighbour; execute the judgment of truth and peace in your gates.   ZECHARIAH 8:16

And ye shall know the truth, and the truth shall make you free.
                                                    JOHN 8:32

For the law was given by Moses, but grace and truth came by Jesus Christ.   JOHN 1:17

God is a Spirit: and they that worship him must worship him in spirit and in truth.   JOHN 4:24

Even the Spirit of truth; whom the world cannot receive, because it seeth him not, neither knoweth him: but ye know him; for he dwelleth with you, and shall be in you.   JOHN 14:17

Truth,

when not sought after,

rarely comes to light.

OLIVER WENDELL HOLMES

For the LORD is good; his mercy is everlasting; and his truth endureth to all generations.   PSALM 100:5

Buy the truth, and sell it not; also wisdom, and instruction, and understanding.   PROVERBS 23:23

Wherefore putting away lying, speak every man truth with his neighbour: for we are members one of another.   EPHESIANS 4:25

Understanding

The noblest pleasure is
the joy of
understanding.

Leonardo da Vinci

Then shalt thou understand the fear of the LORD, and find the knowledge of God. For the LORD giveth wisdom: out of his mouth cometh knowledge and understanding.   Proverbs 2:5–6

If there be therefore any consolation in Christ, if any comfort of love, if any fellowship of the Spirit, if any bowels and mercies, fulfil ye my joy, that ye be likeminded, having the same love, being of one accord, of one mind.   Philippians 2:1–2

When I was a child, I spake as a child, I understood as a child, I thought as a child: but when I became a man, I put away childish things.   1 Corinthians 13:11

The tongue of the wise useth knowledge aright: but the mouth of fools poureth out foolishness. PROVERBS 15:2

Justice and judgment are the habitation of thy throne: mercy and truth shall go before thy face. PSALM 89:14

In the lips of him that hath understanding wisdom is found: but a rod is for the back of him that is void of understanding.
PROVERBS 10:13

With the ancient is wisdom; and in length of days understanding. With him is wisdom and strength, he hath counsel and understanding. JOB 12:12–13

O God,

help us not to despise or oppose

what we do not understand.

WILLIAM PENN

Wisdom resteth in the heart of him that hath understanding: but that which is in the midst of fools is made known.
PROVERBS 14:33

But let him that glorieth glory in this, that he understandeth and knoweth me, that I am the LORD which exercise lovingkindness, judgment, and righteousness, in the earth: for in these things I delight, saith the LORD. JEREMIAH 9:24

Evil men understand not judgment: but they that seek the LORD understand all things. PROVERBS 28:5

But as it is written, Eye hath not seen, nor ear heard, neither have entered into the heart of man, the things which God hath prepared for them that love him. But God hath revealed them unto us by his Spirit: for the Spirit searcheth all things, yea, the deep things of God. For what man knoweth the things of a man, save the spirit of man which is in him? even so the things of God knoweth no man, but the Spirit of God.   1 CORINTHIANS 2:9–11

The heart of the prudent getteth knowledge; and the ear of the wise seeketh knowledge.   PROVERBS 18:15

But thou, O LORD, art a God full of compassion, and gracious, longsuffering, and plenteous in mercy and truth.   PSALM 86:15

Make me to understand the way of thy precepts: so shall I talk of thy wondrous works.   PSALM 119:27

For if these things be in you, and abound, they make you that ye shall neither be barren nor unfruitful in the knowledge of our Lord Jesus Christ.   2 PETER 1:8

And unto man he said, Behold, the fear of the LORD, that is wisdom; and to depart from evil is understanding.   JOB 28:28

Folly is joy to him that is destitute of wisdom: but a man of understanding walketh uprightly.   PROVERBS 15:21

The rich man is wise in his own conceit; but the poor that hath understanding searcheth him out.   PROVERBS 28:11

Teach me good judgment and knowledge: for I have believed thy commandments.   PSALM 119:66

The heart of him that hath understanding seeketh knowledge: but the mouth of fools feedeth on foolishness.   PROVERBS 15:14

When wisdom entereth into thine heart, and knowledge is pleasant unto thy soul; discretion shall preserve thee, understanding shall keep thee: To deliver thee from the way of the evil man.

PROVERBS 2:10–12

For to one is given by the Spirit the word of wisdom; to another the word of knowledge by the same Spirit.   1 CORINTHIANS 12:8

Happy is the man that findeth wisdom, and the man that getteth understanding. For the merchandise of it is better than the merchandise of silver, and the gain thereof than fine gold. She is more precious than rubies: and all the things thou canst desire are not to be compared unto her.   PROVERBS 3:13–15

They shall not hurt nor destroy in all my holy mountain: for the earth shall be full of the knowledge of the LORD, as the waters cover the sea. And in that day there shall be a root of Jesse, which shall stand for an ensign of the people; to it shall the Gentiles seek: and his rest shall be glorious.   ISAIAH 11:9–10

UNITY

What ever disunites
man from God
also disunites man from man.

EDMUND BURKE

Can two walk together, except they be agreed?   AMOS 3:3

Let him seek peace, and ensue it.   1 PETER 3:11

Be of the same mind one toward another.   ROMANS 12:16

Till we all come in the unity of the faith, and of the knowledge of
the Son of God, unto a perfect man, unto the measure of the
stature of the fulness of Christ.   EPHESIANS 4:13

Behold, how good and how pleasant it is for brethren to dwell together in unity!   PSALM 133:1

Has it ever occurred to you that

one hundred pianos all tuned to the same fork

are automatically tuned to each other?

They are of one accord by being tuned, not to each other,

but to another standard to which

each one must individually bow.

So one hundred worshippers meeting together,

each one looking away to Christ,

are in heart nearer to each other than

they could possibly be were they to become

"unity" conscious and turn their eyes away

from God to strive for closer fellowship.

Social religion is perfected when

private religion is purified.

The body becomes stronger as

its members become healthier.

The whole church of God gains when the members

that compose it begin to seek a better and a higher life.

A. W. TOZER

For by one Spirit are we all baptized into one body, whether we be Jews or Gentiles, whether we be bond or free; and have been all made to drink into one Spirit.   1 CORINTHIANS 12:13

But he that is joined unto the Lord is one spirit.
                                                      1 CORINTHIANS 6:17

Now the God of patience and consolation grant you to be like-minded one toward another according to Christ Jesus: That ye may with one mind and one mouth glorify God, even the Father of our Lord Jesus Christ.   ROMANS 15:5–6

I. . .beseech you that ye walk worthy of the vocation wherewith ye are called, with all lowliness and meekness, with longsuffering, forbearing one another in love; endeavouring to keep the unity of the Spirit in the bond of peace. There is one body, and one Spirit, even as ye are called in one hope of your calling; one Lord, one faith, one baptism, one God and Father of all, who is above all, and through all, and in you all.   EPHESIANS 4:1–6

Now I beseech you, brethren, by the name of our Lord Jesus Christ, that ye all speak the same thing, and that there be no divisions among you; but that ye be perfectly joined together in the same mind and in the same judgment.   1 CORINTHIANS 1:10

VIGILANCE

As long as I see any thing
to be done for God,
life is worth having;
but O how vain
and unworthy it is
to live for any lower end!

DAVID BRAINERD

Be sober, be vigilant; because your adversary the devil, as a roaring lion, walketh about, seeking whom he may devour.   1 PETER 5:8

I watch, and am as a sparrow alone upon the house top.

PSALM 102:7

Watch and pray, that ye enter not into temptation: the spirit indeed is willing, but the flesh is weak.   MATTHEW 26:41

Let thine eyes look right on, and let thine eyelids look straight before thee. Ponder the path of thy feet, and let all thy ways be established.   PROVERBS 4:25–26

He that dasheth in pieces is come up before thy face: keep the munition, watch the way, make thy loins strong, fortify thy power mightily.   NAHUM 2:1

I will stand upon my watch, and set me upon the tower, and will watch to see what he will say unto me, and what I shall answer when I am reproved.   HABAKKUK 2:1

Watch therefore: for ye know not what hour your Lord doth come. But know this, that if the goodman of the house had known in what watch the thief would come, he would have watched, and would not have suffered his house to be broken up.
                                                          MATTHEW 24:42–43

And then if any man shall say to you, Lo, here is Christ; or, lo, he is there; believe him not: For false Christs and false prophets shall rise, and shall shew signs and wonders, to seduce, if it were possible, even the elect. But take ye heed: behold, I have foretold you all things.   MARK 13:21–23

And what I say unto you I say unto all, Watch.   MARK 13:37

Beware lest any man spoil you through philosophy and vain deceit, after the tradition of men, after the rudiments of the world, and not after Christ.   COLOSSIANS 2:8

Look to yourselves, that we lose not those things which we have wrought, but that we receive a full reward.   2 JOHN 8

Blessed is the man that heareth me, watching daily at my gates, waiting at the posts of my doors.   PROVERBS 8:34

Let every one consider what his weak point is;

in that is his trial.

His trial is not in those things which are easy to him,

but in that one thing, in those several things,

whatever they are, in which to do

his duty is against his nature.

Never think yourself safe because

you do your duty in ninety-nine points;

it is the hundredth which is to be

the ground of your self-denial.

It is with reference to this you must watch and pray;

pray continually for God's grace to help you,

and watch with fear and trembling lest you fall.

Oh that you may (as it were) sweep the house diligently

to discover what you lack of the full measure of obedience!

for, be quite sure, that this apparently small defect will

influence your whole spirit and judgment in all things.

JOHN HENRY NEWMAN

Watch ye therefore, and pray always, that ye may be accounted worthy to escape all these things that shall come to pass, and to stand before the Son of man.   LUKE 21:36

But watch thou in all things, endure afflictions, do the work of an evangelist, make full proof of thy ministry.   2 TIMOTHY 4:5

WISDOM

Wisdom is the right use of knowledge.
To know is not to be wise.
Many men know a great deal
and are all the greater fools for it.
There is no fool so great a fool
as a knowing fool.
But to know how to use knowledge
is to have wisdom.

CHARLES H. SPURGEON

He that is void of wisdom despiseth his neighbour: but a man of understanding holdeth his peace.   PROVERBS 11:12

I wisdom dwell with prudence, and find out knowledge of witty inventions.   PROVERBS 8:12

Therefore whosoever heareth these sayings of mine, and doeth them, I will liken him unto a wise man, which built his house upon a rock: And the rain descended, and the floods came, and the winds blew, and beat upon that house; and it fell not: for it was founded upon a rock.   MATTHEW 7:24–25

A prudent man foreseeth the evil, and hideth himself: but the simple pass on, and are punished.   PROVERBS 22:3

The LORD by wisdom hath founded the earth; by understanding hath he established the heavens. By his knowledge the depths are broken up, and the clouds drop down the dew. My son, let not them depart from thine eyes: keep sound wisdom and discretion.   PROVERBS 3:19–21

Whoso is wise, and will observe these things, even they shall understand the lovingkindness of the LORD.   PSALM 107:43

A good man sheweth favour, and lendeth: he will guide his affairs with discretion.   PSALM 112:5

He that handleth a matter wisely shall find good: and whoso trusteth in the LORD, happy is he. The wise in heart shall be called prudent: and the sweetness of the lips increaseth learning.   PROVERBS 16:20–21

Who is wise, and he shall understand these things? prudent, and he shall know them? for the ways of the LORD are right, and the just shall walk in them: but the transgressors shall fall therein.   HOSEA 14:9

My son, attend to my words; incline thine ear unto my sayings. Let them not depart from thine eyes; keep them in the midst of thine heart. For they are life unto those that find them, and health to all their flesh.   PROVERBS 4:20–22

A prudent man concealeth knowledge: but the heart of fools pro-claimeth foolishness.
PROVERBS 12:23

A wise man's heart discerneth both time and judgment.
ECCLESIASTES 8:5

I wish to show that there is

one wisdom which is perfect,

and that this is contained in the scriptures.

ROGER BACON

Be wise now therefore, O ye kings: be instructed, ye judges of the earth.
PSALM 2:10

The simple believeth every word: but the prudent man looketh well to his going.
PROVERBS 14:15

Say unto wisdom, Thou art my sister; and call understanding thy kinswoman.
PROVERBS 7:4

Wherefore be ye not unwise, but understanding what the will of the Lord is.
EPHESIANS 5:17

The law of the wise is a fountain of life, to depart from the snares of death. Good understanding giveth favour: but the way of trans-gressors is hard.
PROVERBS 13:14–15

For your obedience is come abroad unto all men. I am glad there-fore on your behalf: but yet I would have you wise unto that which is good, and simple concerning evil.
ROMANS 16:19

How much better is it to get wisdom than gold! and to get under-standing rather to be chosen than silver!   PROVERBS 16:16

And they that be wise shall shine as the brightness of the firma-ment; and they that turn many to righteousness as the stars for ever and ever.   DANIEL 12:3

With him is strength and wisdom: the deceived and the deceiver are his. He leadeth counsellors away spoiled, and maketh the judges fools.   JOB 12:16–17

And wisdom and knowledge shall be the stability of thy times, and strength of salvation: the fear of the LORD is his treasure.
    ISAIAH 33:6

If any of you lack wisdom, let him ask of God, that giveth to all men liberally, and upbraideth not; and it shall be given him.
    JAMES 1:5

My son, eat thou honey, because it is good; and the honeycomb, which is sweet to thy taste: So shall the knowledge of wisdom be unto thy soul: when thou hast found it, then there shall be a reward, and thy expectation shall not be cut off.   PROVERBS 24:13–14

I will instruct thee and teach thee in the way which thou shalt go: I will guide thee with mine eye.   PSALM 32:8

And if any man think that he knoweth any thing, he knoweth nothing yet as he ought to know.   1 CORINTHIANS 8:2

And he will teach us of his ways, and we will walk in his paths.
    ISAIAH 2:3

For God giveth to a man that is good in his sight wisdom, and knowledge, and joy.   ECCLESIASTES 2:26

Howbeit we speak wisdom among them that are perfect: yet not the wisdom of this world, nor of the princes of this world, that come to nought: But we speak the wisdom of God in a mystery, even the hidden wisdom, which God ordained before the world unto our glory: Which none of the princes of this world knew: for had they known it, they would not have crucified the Lord of glory.

1 CORINTHIANS 2:6–8

Wisdom is, and starts with,

the humility to accept the fact

that you don't have all the right answers

and the courage to learn to ask the right questions.

ANONYMOUS

For God, who commanded the light to shine out of darkness, hath shined in our hearts, to give the light of the knowledge of the glory of God in the face of Jesus Christ. 2 CORINTHIANS 4:6

Then shalt thou understand the fear of the LORD, and find the knowledge of God. For the LORD giveth wisdom: out of his mouth cometh knowledge and understanding. He layeth up sound wisdom for righteous: he is a buckler to them that walk uprightly.

PROVERBS 2:5–7

I will bless the LORD, who hath given me counsel: my reins also instruct me in the night seasons. PSALM 16:7

Evil men understand not judgment: but they that seek the LORD understand all things. PROVERBS 28:5

And we know that the Son of God is come, and hath given us an understanding, that we may know him that is true, and we are in him that is true, even in his Son Jesus Christ. This is the true God, and eternal life.   1 JOHN 5:20

Behold, thou desirest truth in the inward parts: and in the hidden part thou shalt make me to know wisdom.   PSALM 51:6

WORK

*Big jobs usually go
to the men who prove
their ability to
outgrow small ones.*

RALPH WALDO EMERSON

He becometh poor that dealeth with a slack hand: but the hand of the diligent maketh rich.   PROVERBS 10:4

The soul of the sluggard desireth, and hath nothing: but the soul of the diligent shall be made fat.   PROVERBS 13:4

Not slothful in business; fervent in spirit; serving the Lord.
                    ROMANS 12:11

The hand of the diligent shall bear rule: but the slothful shall be under tribute.   PROVERBS 12:24

But if any provide not for his own, and specially for those of his own house, he hath denied the faith, and is worse than an infidel.

1 TIMOTHY 5:8

Whatsoever thy hand findeth to do, do it with thy might; for there is no work, nor device, nor knowledge, nor wisdom, in the grave, whither thou goest.   ECCLESIASTES 9:10

Let him that stole steal no more: but rather let him labour, working with his hands the thing which is good, that he may have to give to him that needeth.   EPHESIANS 4:28

He that tilleth his land shall be satisfied with bread: but he that followeth vain persons is void of understanding.   PROVERBS 12:11

For even when we were with you, this we commanded you, that if any would not work, neither should he eat. For we hear that there are some which walk among you disorderly, working not at all, but are busybodies. Now them that are such we command and exhort by our Lord Jesus Christ, that with quietness they work, and eat their own bread.   2 THESSALONIANS 3:10–12

And that ye study to be quiet, and to do your own business, and to work with your own hands, as we commanded you; that ye may walk honestly toward them that are without, and that ye may have lack of nothing.   1 THESSALONIANS 4:11–12

There be four things which are little upon the earth, but they are exceeding wise. . . . The spider taketh hold with her hands, and is in kings' palaces.   PROVERBS 30:24, 28

I know that there is no good in them, but for a man to rejoice, and to do good in his life. And also that every man should eat and drink, and enjoy the good of all his labour, it is the gift of God.

ECCLESIASTES 3:12–13

Love not sleep, lest thou come to poverty; open thine eyes, and thou shalt be satisfied with bread.   Proverbs 20:13

Wealth gotten by vanity shall be diminished: but he that gathereth by labour shall increase.   Proverbs 13:11

Things may come to those who wait,

but only the things left by

those who hustle.

Abraham Lincoln

Then said they unto him, What shall we do, that we might work the works of God? Jesus answered and said unto them, This is the work of God, that ye believe on him whom he hath sent.
                                                          John 6:28–29

And God blessed the seventh day, and sanctified it: because that in it he had rested from all his work which God created and made.
                                                          Genesis 2:3

The Lord shall open unto thee his good treasure, the heaven to give the rain unto thy land in his season, and to bless all the work of thine hand: and thou shalt lend unto many nations, and thou shalt not borrow.   Deuteronomy 28:12

For thou shalt eat the labour of thine hands: happy shalt thou be, and it shall be well with thee.   Psalm 128:2

Be ye strong therefore, and let not your hands be weak: for your work shall be rewarded.   2 Chronicles 15:7

Therefore, my beloved brethren, be ye stedfast, unmoveable, always abounding in the work of the Lord, forasmuch as ye know that your labour is not in vain in the Lord.   1 CORINTHIANS 15:58

And in every work that he began in the service of the house of God, and in the law, and in the commandments, to seek his God, he did it with all his heart, and prospered.   2 CHRONICLES 31:21

Even a child is known by his doings, whether his work be pure, and whether it be right.   PROVERBS 20:11

I have glorified thee on the earth: I have finished the work which thou gavest me to do.   JOHN 17:4

That ye might walk worthy of the Lord unto all pleasing, being fruitful in every good work, and increasing in the knowledge of God.   COLOSSIANS 1:10

Opportunity is missed

by most people because

it is dressed in overalls

and looks like work.

THOMAS EDISON

In all labour there is profit: but the talk of the lips tendeth only to penury.   PROVERBS 14:23

Come unto me, all ye that labour and are heavy laden, and I will give you rest.   MATTHEW 11:28

Except the LORD build the house, they labour in vain that build it: except the LORD keep the city, the watchman waketh but in vain.

PSALM 127:1

For God is not unrighteous to forget your work and labour of love, which ye have shewed toward his name, in that ye have ministered to the saints, and do minister. And we desire that every one of you do shew the same diligence to the full assurance of hope unto the end.

HEBREWS 6:10–11

WORRY

*It only seems as if you are doing
something when you're worrying.*

LUCY MAUD MONTGOMERY

Be careful for nothing; but in every thing by prayer and supplication with thanksgiving let your requests be made known unto
God. And the peace of God, which passeth all understanding, shall
keep your hearts and minds through Christ Jesus.

PHILIPPIANS 4:6–7

For he shall be as a tree planted by the waters, and that spreadeth
out her roots by the river, and shall not see when heat cometh, but
her leaf shall be green; and shall not be careful in the year of
drought, neither shall cease from yielding fruit.   JEREMIAH 17:8

But my God shall supply all your need according to his riches in
glory by Christ Jesus.   PHILIPPIANS 4:19

God is our refuge and strength, a very present help in trouble. Therefore will not we fear, though the earth be removed, and though the
mountains be carried into the midst of the sea; though the waters
thereof roar and be troubled, though the mountains shake with the
swelling thereof.   PSALM 46:1–3

And Jesus answered and said unto her, Martha, Martha, thou art
careful and troubled about many things: But one thing is needful:
and Mary hath chosen that good part, which shall not be taken
away from her.   LUKE 10:41–42

Any concern too small

to be turned into a prayer is to

small to be made into a burden.

CORRIE TEN BOOM

The LORD also will be a refuge for the oppressed, a refuge in times
of trouble. And they that know thy name will put their trust in
thee: for thou, LORD, hast not forsaken them that seek thee.
                                                       PSALM 9:9–10

Thou art my hiding place; thou shalt preserve me from trouble;
thou shalt compass me about with songs of deliverance.
                                                       PSALM 32:7

He shall call upon me, and I will answer him: I will be with him
in trouble; I will deliver him, and honour him.   PSALM 91:15

And the work of righteousness shall be peace; and the effect of
righteousness quietness and assurance for ever.   ISAIAH 32:17

We are troubled on every side, yet not distressed; we are perplexed, but not in despair; persecuted, but not forsaken; cast down, but not destroyed.   2 CORINTHIANS 4:8–9

Therefore I say unto you, Take no thought for your life, what ye shall eat, or what ye shall drink; nor yet for your body, what ye shall put on. Is not the life more than meat, and the body than raiment? Behold the fowls of the air: for they sow not, neither do they reap, nor gather into barns; yet your heavenly Father feedeth them. Are ye not much better than they? Which of you by taking thought can add one cubit unto his stature? And why take ye thought for raiment? Consider the lilies of the field, how they grow; they toil not, neither do they spin: And yet I say unto you, That even Solomon in all his glory was not arrayed like one of these. Wherefore, if God so clothe the grass of the field, which to day is, and to morrow is cast into the oven, shall he not much more clothe you, O ye of little faith? Therefore take no thought, saying, What shall we eat? or, What shall we drink? or, Wherewithal shall we be clothed? (For after all these things do the Gentiles seek:) for your heavenly Father knoweth that ye have need of all these things. But seek ye first the kingdom of God, and his righteousness; and all these things shall be added unto you. Take therefore no thought for the morrow: for the morrow shall take thought for the things of itself. Sufficient unto the day is the evil thereof.
                                                    MATTHEW 6:25–34

But when they shall lead you, and deliver you up, take no thought beforehand what ye shall speak, neither do ye premeditate: but whatsoever shall be given you in that hour, that speak ye: for it is not ye that speak, but the Holy Ghost.   MARK 13:11

And when they bring you unto the synagogues, and unto magistrates, and powers, take ye no thought how or what thing ye shall answer, or what ye shall say: For the Holy Ghost shall teach you in the same hour what ye ought to say.   LUKE 12:11–12

SCHEDULE FOR READING
THROUGH THE BIBLE IN A YEAR

Bible Readings for January

January 1 - Luke 5:27–39, Genesis 1–2, Psalm 1
January 2 - Luke 6:1–26, Genesis 3–5, Psalm 2
January 3 - Luke 6:27–49, Genesis 6–7, Psalm 3
January 4 - Luke 7:1–17, Genesis 8–10, Psalm 4
January 5 - Luke 7:18–50, Genesis 11, Psalm 5
January 6 - Luke 8:1–25, Genesis 12, Psalm 6
January 7 - Luke 8:26–56, Genesis 13–14, Psalm 7
January 8 - Luke 9:1–27, Genesis 15, Psalm 8
January 9 - Luke 9:28–62, Genesis 16, Psalm 9
January 10 - Luke 10:1–20, Genesis 17, Psalm 10
January 11 - Luke 10:21–42, Genesis 18, Psalm 11
January 12 - Luke 11:1–28, Genesis 19, Psalm 12
January 13 - Luke 11:29–54, Genesis 20, Psalm 13
January 14 - Luke 12:1–31, Genesis 21, Psalm 14
January 15 - Luke 12:32–59, Genesis 22, Psalm 15
January 16 - Luke 13:1–17, Genesis 23, Psalm 16
January 17 - Luke 13:18–35, Genesis 24, Psalm 17
January 18 - Luke 14:1–24, Genesis 25, Psalm 18
January 19 - Luke 14:25–35, Genesis 26, Psalm 19
January 20 - Luke 15, Genesis 27:1–45, Psalm 20
January 21 - Luke 16, Genesis 27:46–28:22, Psalm 21
January 22 - Luke 17, Genesis 29:1–30, Psalm 22
January 23 - Luke 18:1–17, Genesis 29:31–30:43, Psalm 23
January 24 - Luke 18:18–43, Genesis 31, Psalm 24
January 25 - Luke 19:1–27, Genesis 32–33, Psalm 25
January 26 - Luke 19:28–48, Genesis 34, Psalm 26
January 27 - Luke 20:1–26, Genesis 35–36, Psalm 27
January 28 - Luke 20:27–47, Genesis 37, Psalm 28
January 29 - Luke 21, Genesis 38, Psalm 29
January 30 - Luke 22:1–38, Genesis 39, Psalm 30
January 31 - Luke 22:39–71, Genesis 40, Psalm 31

Bible Readings for February

February 1 - Luke 23:1–25, Genesis 41, Psalm 32
February 2 - Luke 23:26–56, Genesis 42, Psalm 33
February 3 - Luke 24:1–12, Genesis 43, Psalm 34
February 4 - Luke 24:13–53, Genesis 44, Psalm 35
February 5 - Hebrews 1, Genesis 45:1–46:27, Psalm 36

February 6 - Hebrews 2, Genesis 46:28–47:31, Psalm 37
February 7 - Hebrews 3:1–4:13, Genesis 48, Psalm 38
February 8 - Hebrews 4:14–6:12, Genesis 49–50, Psalm 39
February 9 - Hebrews 6:13–20, Exodus 1–2, Psalm 40
February 10 - Hebrews 7, Exodus 3–4, Psalm 41
February 11 - Hebrews 8, Exodus 5:1–6:27, Proverbs 1
February 12 - Hebrews 9:1–22, Exodus 6:28–8:32, Proverbs 2
February 13 - Hebrews 9:23–10:18, Exodus 9–10, Proverbs 3
February 14 - Hebrews 10:19–39, Exodus 11–12, Proverbs 4
February 15 - Hebrews 11:1–22, Exodus 13–14, Proverbs 5
February 16 - Hebrews 11:23–40, Exodus 15, Proverbs 6:1–7:5
February 17 - Hebrews 12, Exodus 16–17, Proverbs 7:6–27
February 18 - Hebrews 13, Exodus 18–19, Proverbs 8
February 19 - Matthew 1, Exodus 20–21, Proverbs 9
February 20 - Matthew 2, Exodus 22–23, Proverbs 10
February 21 - Matthew 3, Exodus 24, Proverbs 11
February 22 - Matthew 4, Exodus 25–27, Proverbs 12
February 23 - Matthew 5:1–20, Exodus 28–29, Proverbs 13
February 24 - Matthew 5:21–48, Exodus 30–32, Proverbs 14
February 25 - Matthew 6:1–18, Exodus 33–34, Proverbs 15
February 26 - Matthew 6:19–34, Exodus 35–36, Proverbs 16
February 27 - Matthew 7, Exodus 37–38, Proverbs 17
February 28 - Matthew 8:1–13, Exodus 39–40, Proverbs 18

Bible Readings for March

March 1 - Matthew 8:14–34, Leviticus 1–2, Proverbs 19
March 2 - Matthew 9:1–17, Leviticus 3–4, Proverbs 20
March 3 - Matthew 9:18–38, Leviticus 5–6, Proverbs 21
March 4 - Matthew 10:1–25, Leviticus 7–8, Proverbs 22
March 5 - Matthew 10:26–42, Leviticus 9–10, Proverbs 23
March 6 - Matthew 11:1–19, Leviticus 11–12, Proverbs 24
March 7 - Matthew 11:20–30, Leviticus 13, Proverbs 25
March 8 - Matthew 12:1–21, Leviticus 14, Proverbs 26
March 9 - Matthew 12:22–50, Leviticus 15–16, Proverbs 27
March 10 - Matthew 13:1–23, Leviticus 17–18, Proverbs 28
March 11 - Matthew 13:24–58, Leviticus 19, Proverbs 29
March 12 - Matthew 14:1–21, Leviticus 20–21, Proverbs 30
March 13 - Matthew 14:22–36, Leviticus 22–23, Proverbs 31
March 14 - Matthew 15:1–20, Leviticus 24–25, Ecclesiastes 1:1–11
March 15 - Matthew 15:21–39, Leviticus 26–27, Ecclesiastes 1:12–2:26
March 16 - Matthew 16, Numbers 1–2, Ecclesiastes 3:1–15
March 17 - Matthew 17, Numbers 3–4, Ecclesiastes 3:16–4:16
March 18 - Matthew 18:1–20, Numbers 5–6, Ecclesiastes 5
March 19 - Matthew 18:21–35, Numbers 7–8, Ecclesiastes 6
March 20 - Matthew 19:1–15, Numbers 9–10, Ecclesiastes 7

March 21 - Matthew 19:16–30, Numbers 11–12, Ecclesiastes 8
March 22 - Matthew 20:1–16, Numbers 13–14, Ecclesiastes 9:1–12
March 23 - Matthew 20:17–34, Numbers 15–16, Ecclesiastes 9:13–10:20
March 24 - Matthew 21:1–27, Numbers 17–18, Ecclesiastes 11:1–8
March 25 - Matthew 21:28–46, Numbers 19–20, Ecclesiastes 11:9–12:14
March 26 - Matthew 22:1–22, Numbers 21, Song of Solomon 1:1–2:7
March 27 - Matthew 22:23–46, Numbers 22:1–40, Song of Solomon 2:8-3:5
March 28 - Matthew 23:1–12, Numbers 22:41–23:26, Song of Solomon 3:6–5:1
March 29 - Matthew 23:13–39, Numbers 23:27–24:25, Song of Solomon 5:2–6:3
March 30 - Matthew 24:1–31, Numbers 25–27, Song of Solomon 6:4–8:4
March 31 - Matthew 24:32–51, Numbers 28–29, Song of Solomon 8:5–14

Bible Readings for April
April 1 - Matthew 25:1–30, Numbers 30–31, Job 1
April 2 - Matthew 25:31–46, Numbers 32–34, Job 2
April 3 - Matthew 26:1–25, Numbers 35–36, Job 3
April 4 - Matthew 26:26–46, Deuteronomy 1–2, Job 4
April 5 - Matthew 26:47–75, Deuteronomy 3–4, Job 5
April 6 - Matthew 27:1–31, Deuteronomy 5–6, Job 6
April 7 - Matthew 27:32–66, Deuteronomy 7–8, Job 7
April 8 - Matthew 28, Deuteronomy 9–10, Job 8
April 9 - Acts 1, Deuteronomy 11–12, Job 9
April 10 - Acts 2:1–13, Deuteronomy 13–14, Job 10
April 11 - Acts 2:14–47, Deuteronomy 15–16, Job 11
April 12 - Acts 3, Deuteronomy 17–18, Job 12
April 13 - Acts 4:1–22, Deuteronomy 19–20, Job 13
April 14 - Acts 4:23–37, Deuteronomy 21–22, Job 14
April 15 - Acts 5:1–16, Deuteronomy 23–24, Job 15
April 16 - Acts 5:17–42, Deuteronomy 25–27, Job 16
April 17 - Acts 6, Deuteronomy 28, Job 17
April 18 - Acts 7:1–22, Deuteronomy 29–30, Job 18
April 19 - Acts 7:23–60, Deuteronomy 31–32, Job 19
April 20 - Acts 8:1–25, Deuteronomy 33–34, Job 20
April 21 - Acts 8:26–40, Joshua 1–2, Job 21
April 22 - Aets 9:1–25, Joshua 3:1–5:1, Job 22
April 23 - Acts 9:26–43, Joshua 5:2–6:27, Job 23
April 24 - Acts 10:1–33, Joshua 7–8, Job 24
April 25 - Acts 10:34–48, Joshua 9–10, Job 25
April 26 - Acts 11:1–18, Joshua 11–12, Job 26
April 27 - Acts 11:19–30, Joshua 13–14, Job 27
April 28 - Acts 12, Joshua 15–17, Job 28
April 29 - Acts 13:1–25, Joshua 18–19, Job 29
April 30 - Acts 13:26–52, Joshua 20–21, Job 30

Bible Readings for May

May 1 - Acts 14, Joshua 22, Job 31
May 2 - Acts 15:1–21, Joshua 23–24, Job 32
May 3 - Acts 15:22–41, Judges 1, Job 33
May 4 - Acts 16:1–15, Judges 2–3, Job 34
May 5 - Acts 16:16–40, Judges 4–5, Job 35
May 6 - Acts 17:1–15, Judges 6, Job 36
May 7 - Acts 17:16–34, Judges 7–8, Job 37
May 8 - Acts 18, Judges 9, Job 38
May 9 - Acts 19:1–20, Judges 10:1–11:33, Job 39
May 10 - Acts 19:21–41, Judges 11:34–12:15, Job 40
May 11 - Acts 20:1–16, Judges 13, Job 41
May 12 - Acts 20:17–38, Judges 14–15, Job 42
May 13 - Acts 21:1–36, Judges 16, Psalm 42
May 14 - Acts 21:37–22:29, Judges 17–18, Psalm 43
May 15 - Acts 22:30–23:22, Judges 19, Psalm 44
May 16 - Acts 23:23–24:9, Judges 20, Psalm 45
May 17 - Acts 24:10–27, Judges 21, Psalm 46
May 18 - Acts 25, Ruth 1–2, Psalm 47
May 19 - Acts 26:1–18, Ruth 3–4, Psalm 48
May 20 - Acts 26:19–32, 1 Samuel 1:1–2:10, Psalm 49
May 21 - Acts 27:1–12, 1 Samuel 2:11–36, Psalm 50
May 22 - Acts 27:13–44, 1 Samuel 3, Psalm 51
May 23 - Acts 28:1–16, 1 Samuel 4–5, Psalm 52
May 24 - Acts 28:17–31, 1 Samuel 6–7, Psalm 53
May 25 - Romans 1:1–15, 1 Samuel 8, Psalm 54
May 26 - Romans 1:16–32, 1 Samuel 9:1–10:16, Psalm 55
May 27 - Romans 2:1–3:8, 1 Samuel 10:17–11:15, Psalm 56
May 28 - Romans 3:9–31, 1 Samuel 12, Psalm 57
May 29 - Romans 4, 1 Samuel 13, Psalm 58
May 30 - Romans 5, 1 Samuel 14, Psalm 59
May 31 - Romans 6, 1 Samuel 15, Psalm 60

Bible Readings for June

June 1 - Romans 7, 1 Samuel 16, Psalm 61
June 2 - Romans 8 1 Samuel 17:1–54, Psalm 62
June 3 - Romans 9:1–29, 1 Samuel 17:55–18:30, Psalm 63
June 4 - Romans 9:30–10:21, 1 Samuel 19, Psalm 64
June 5 - Romans 11:1–24, 1 Samuel 20, Psalm 65
June 6 - Romans 11:25–36, 1 Samuel 21–22, Psalm 66
June 7 - Romans 12, 1 Samuel 23–24, Psalm 67
June 8 - Romans 13, 1 Samuel 25, Psalm 68
June 9 - Romans 14, 1 Samuel 26, Psalm 69
June 10 - Romans 15:1–13, 1 Samuel 27–28, Psalm 70
June 11 - Romans 15:14–33, 1 Samuel 29–31, Psalm 71

June 12 - Romans 16, 2 Samuel 1, Psalm 72
June 13 - Mark 1:1–20, 2 Samuel 2:1–3:1, Daniel 1
June 14 - Mark 1:21–45, 2 Samuel 3:2–39, Daniel 2:1–23
June 15 - Mark 2, 2 Samuel 4–5, Daniel 2:24–49
June 16 - Mark 3:1–19, 2 Samuel 6, Daniel 3
June 17 - Mark 3:20–35, 2 Samuel 7–8, Daniel 4
June 18 - Mark 4:1–20, 2 Samuel 9–10, Daniel 5
June 19 - Mark 4:21–41, 2 Samuel 11–12, Daniel 6
June 20 - Mark 5:1–20, 2 Samuel 13, Daniel 7
June 21 - Mark 5:21–43, 2 Samuel 14, Daniel 8
June 22 - Mark 6:1–29, 2 Samuel 15, Daniel 9
June 23 - Mark 6:30–56, 2 Samuel 16, Daniel 10
June 24 - Mark 7:1–13, 2 Samuel 17, Daniel 11:1–19
June 25 - Mark 7:14–37, 2 Samuel 18, Daniel 11:20–45
June 26 - Mark 8:1–21, 2 Samuel 19, Daniel 12
June 27 - Mark 8:22–9:1, 2 Samuel 20–21, Hosea 1:1–2:1
June 28 - Mark 9:2–50, 2 Samuel 22, Hosea 2:2–23
June 29 - Mark 10:1–31, 2 Samuel 23, Hosea 3
June 30 - Mark 10:32–52, 2 Samuel 24, Hosea 4:1–11

Bible Readings for July
July 1 - Mark 11:1–14, 1 Kings 1, Hosea 4:12–5:4
July 2 - Mark 11:15–33, 1 Kings 2, Hosea 5:5–15
July 3 - Mark 12:1–27, 1 Kings 3, Hosea 6:1–7:2
July 4 - Mark 12:28–44, 1 Kings 4-5, Hosea 7:3–16
July 5 - Mark 13:1–13, 1 Kings 6, Hosea 8
July 6 - Mark 13:14–37, 1 Kings 7, Hosea 9:1–16
July 7 - Mark 14:1–31, 1 Kings 8, Hosea 9:17–10:15
July 8 - Mark 14:32–72, 1 Kings 9, Hosea 11:1–11
July 9 - Mark 15:1–20, 1 Kings 10, Hosea 11:12–12:14
July 10 - Mark 15:21–47, 1 Kings 11, Hosea 13
July 11 - Mark 16, 1 Kings 12:1–31, Hosea 14
July 12 - 1 Corinthians 1:1–17, 1 Kings 12:32–13:34, Joel 1
July 13 - 1 Corinthians 1:18–31, 1 Kings 14, Joel 2:1–11
July 14 - 1 Corinthians 2, 1 Kings 15:1–32, Joel 2:12–32
July 15 - 1 Corinthians 3, 1 Kings 15:33–16:34, Joel 3
July 16 - 1 Corinthians 4, 1 Kings 17, Amos 1
July 17 - 1 Corinthians 5, 1 Kings 18, Amos 2:1–3:2
July 18 - 1 Corinthians 6, 1 Kings 19, Amos 3:3–4:3
July 19 - 1 Corinthians 7:1–24, 1 Kings 20, Amos 4:4–13
July 20 - 1 Corinthians 7:25–40, 1 Kings 21, Amos 5
July 21 - 1 Corinthians 8, 1 Kings 22, Amos 6
July 22 - 1 Corinthians 9, 2 Kings 1–2, Amos 7
July 23 - 1 Corinthians 10, 2 Kings 3, Amos 8
July 24 - 1 Corinthians 11:1–16, 2 Kings 4, Amos 9

July 25 - 1 Corinthians 11:17–34, 2 Kings 5, Obadiah
July 26 - 1 Corinthians 12, 2 Kings 6:1–7:2, Jonah 1
July 27 - 1 Corinthians 13, 2 Kings 7:3–20, Jonah 2
July 28 - 1 Corinthians 14:1–25, 2 Kings 8, Jonah 3
July 29 - 1 Corinthians 14:26–40, 2 Kings 9, Jonah 4
July 30 - 1 Corinthians 15:1–34, 2 Kings 10, Micah 1
July 31 - 1 Corinthians 15:35–58, 2 Kings 11, Micah 2

Bible Readings for August

August 1 - 1 Corinthians 16, 2 Kings 12–13, Micah 3
August 2 - 2 Corinthians 1:1–2:4, 2 Kings 14, Micah 4:1–5:1
August 3 - 2 Corinthians 2:5–3:18, 2 Kings 15–16, Micah 5:2–15
August 4 - 2 Corinthians 4:1–5:10, 2 Kings 17, Micah 6
August 5 - 2 Corinthians 5:11–6:13, 2 Kings 18, Micah 7
August 6 - 2 Corinthians 6:14–7:16, 2 Kings 19, Nahum 1
August 7 - 2 Corinthians 8, 2 Kings 20–21, Nahum 2
August 8 - 2 Corinthians 9, 2 Kings 22:1–23:35, Nahum 3
August 9 - 2 Corinthians 10, 2 Kings 23:36–24:20, Habakkuk 1
August 10 - 2 Corinthians 11, 2 Kings 25, Habakkuk 2
August 11 - 2 Corinthians 12, 1 Chronicles 1–2, Habakkuk 3
August 12 - 2 Corinthians 13, 1 Chronicles 3–4, Zephaniah 1
August 13 - John 1:1–18, 1 Chronicles 5–6, Zephaniah 2
August 14 - John 1:19–34, 1 Chronicles 7–8, Zephaniah 3
August 15 - John 1:35–51, 1 Chronicles 9, Haggai 1–2
August 16 - John 2, 1 Chronicles 10–11, Zechariah 1
August 17 - John 3:1–21, 1 Chronicles 12, Zechariah 2
August 18 - John 3:22–36, 1 Chronicles 13–14, Zechariah 3
August 19 - John 4:1–26, 1 Chronicles 15:1–16:6, Zechariah 4
August 20 - John 4:27–42, 1 Chronicles 16:7–43, Zechariah 5
August 21 - John 4:43–54, 1 Chronicles 17, Zechariah 6
August 22 - John 5:1–18, 1 Chronicles 18–19, Zechariah 7
August 23 - John 5:19–47, 1 Chronicles 20:1–22:1, Zechariah 8
August 24 - John 6:1–21, 1 Chronicles 22:2–23:32, Zechariah 9
August 25 - John 6:22–59, 1 Chronicles 24, Zechariah 10
August 26 - John 6:60–71, 1 Chronicles 25–26, Zechariah 11
August 27 - John 7:1–24, 1 Chronicles 27–28, Zechariah 12
August 28 - John 7:25–52, 1 Chronicles 29, Zechariah 13
August 29 - John 8:1–20, 2 Chronicles 1:1–2:16, Zechariah 14
August 30 - John 8:21–47, 2 Chronicles 2:17–5:1, Malachi 1:1–2:9
August 31 - John 8:48–59, 2 Chronicles 5:2–14, Malachi 2:10–16

Bible Readings for September

September 1 - John 9:1–23, 2 Chronicles 6, Malachi 2:17–3:18
September 2 - John 9:24–41, 2 Chronicles 7, Malachi 4
September 3 - John 10:1–21, 2 Chronicles 8, Psalm 73

September 4 - John 10:22–42, 2 Chronicles 9, Psalm 74
September 5 - John 11:1–27, 2 Chronicles 10–11, Psalm 75
September 6 - John 11:28–57, 2 Chronicles 12–13, Psalm 76
September 7 - John 12:1–26, 2 Chronicles 14–15, Psalm 77
September 8 - John 12:27–50, 2 Chronicles 16–17, Psalm 78:1–20
September 9 - John 13:1–20, 2 Chronicles 18, Psalm 78:21–37
September 10 - John 13:21–38, 2 Chronicles 19, Psalm 78:38–55
September 11 - John 14:1–14, 2 Chronicles 20:1–21:1, Psalm 78:56–72
September 12 - John 14:15–31, 2 Chronicles 21:2–22:12, Psalm 79
September 13 - John 15:1–16:4, 2 Chronicles 23, Psalm 80
September 14 - John 16:4–33, 2 Chronicles 24, Psalm 81
September 15 - John 17, 2 Chronicles 25, Psalm 82
September 16 - John 18:1–18, 2 Chronicles 26, Psalm 83
September 17 - John 18:19–38, 2 Chronicles 27–28, Psalm 84
September 18 - John 18:38–19:16, 2 Chronicles 29, Psalm 85
September 19 - John 19:16–42, 2 Chronicles 30, Psalm 86
September 20 - John 20:1–18, 2 Chronicles 31, Psalm 87
September 21 - John 20:19–31, 2 Chronicles 32, Psalm 88
September 22 - John 21, 2 Chronicles 33, Psalm 89:1–18
September 23 - 1 John 1, 2 Chronicles 34, Psalm 89:19–37
September 24 - 1 John 2, 2 Chronicles 35, Psalm 89:38–52
September 25 - 1 John 3, 2 Chronicles 36, Psalm 90
September 26 - 1 John 4, Ezra 1–2, Psalm 91
September 27 - 1 John 5, Ezra 3–4, Psalm 92
September 28 - 2 John, Ezra 5–6, Psalm 93
September 29 - 3 John, Ezra 7–8, Psalm 94
September 30 - Jude, Ezra 9–10, Psalm 95

Bible Readings for October

October 1 - Revelation 1, Nehemiah 1–2, Psalm 96
October 2 - Revelation 2, Nehemiah 3, Psalm 97
October 3 - Revelation 3, Nehemiah 4, Psalm 98
October 4 - Revelation 4, Nehemiah 5:1–7:4, Psalm 99
October 5 - Revelation 5, Nehemiah 7:5–8:12, Psalm 100
October 6 - Revelation 6, Nehemiah 8:13–9:37, Psalm 101
October 7 - Revelation 7, Nehemiah 9:38–10:39, Psalm 102
October 8 - Revelation 8, Nehemiah 11, Psalm 103
October 9 - Revelation 9, Nehemiah 12, Psalm 104:1–23
October 10 - Revelation 10, Nehemiah 13, Psalm 104:24–35
October 11 - Revelation 11, Esther 1, Psalm 105:1–25
October 12 - Revelation 12, Esther 2, Psalm 105:26–45
October 13 - Revelation 13, Esther 3–4, Psalm 106:1–23
October 14 - Revelation 14, Esther 5:1–6:13, Psalm 106:24–48
October 15 - Revelation 15, Esther 6:14–8:17, Psalm 107:1–22
October 16 - Revelation 16, Esther 9–10, Psalm 107:23–43

October 17 - Revelation 17, Isaiah 1–2, Psalm 108
October 18 - Revelation 18, Isaiah 3–4, Psalm 109:1–19
October 19 - Revelation 19, Isaiah 5–6, Psalm 109:20–31
October 20 - Revelation 20, Isaiah 7–8, Psalm 110
October 21 - Revelation 21–22, Isaiah 9–10, Psalm 111
October 22 - 1 Thessalonians 1, Isaiah 11–13, Psalm 112
October 23 - 1 Thessalonians 2:1–16, Isaiah 14–16, Psalm 113
October 24 - 1 Thessalonians 2:17–3:13, Isaiah 17–19, Psalm 114
October 25 - 1 Thessalonians 4, Isaiah 20–22, Psalm 115
October 26 - 1 Thessalonians 5, Isaiah 23–24, Psalm 116
October 27 - 2 Thessalonians 1, Isaiah 25–26, Psalm 117
October 28 - 2 Thessalonians 2, Isaiah 27–28, Psalm 118
October 29 - 2 Thessalonians 3, Isaiah 29–30, Psalm 119:1–32
October 30 - 1 Timothy 1, Isaiah 31–33, Psalm 119:33–64
October 31 - 1 Timothy 2, Isaiah 34–35, Psalm 119:65–96

Bible Readings for November
November 1 - 1 Timothy 3, Isaiah 36–37, Psalm 119:97–120
November 2 - 1 Timothy 4, Isaiah 38–39, Psalm 119:121–144
November 3 - 1 Timothy 5:1–22, Jeremiah 1–2, Psalm 119:145–176
November 4 - 1 Timothy 5:23–6:21, Jeremiah 3–4, Psalm 120
November 5 - 2 Timothy 1, Jeremiah 5–6, Psalm 121
November 6 - 2 Timothy 2, Jeremiah 7–8, Psalm 122
November 7 - 2 Timothy 3, Jeremiah 9–10, Psalm 123
November 8 - 2 Timothy 4, Jeremiah 11–12, Psalm 124
November 9 - Titus 1, Jeremiah 13–14, Psalm 125
November 10 - Titus 2, Jeremiah 15–16, Psalm 126
November 11 - Titus 3, Jeremiah 17–18, Psalm 127
November 12 - Philemon, Jeremiah 19–20, Psalm 128
November 13 - James 1, Jeremiah 21–22, Psalm 129
November 14 - James 2, Jeremiah 23–24, Psalm 130
November 15 - James 3, Jeremiah 25–26, Psalm 131
November 16 - James 4, Jeremiah 27–28, Psalm 132
November 17 - James 5, Jeremiah 29–30, Psalm 133
November 18 - 1 Peter 1, Jeremiah 31–32, Psalm 134
November 19 - 1 Peter 2, Jeremiah 33–34, Psalm 135
November 20 - 1 Peter 3, Jeremiah 35–36, Psalm 136
November 21 - 1 Peter 4, Jeremiah 37–38, Psalm 137
November 22 - 1 Peter 5, Jeremiah 39–40, Psalm 138
November 23 - 2 Peter 1, Jeremiah 41–42, Psalm 139
November 24 - 2 Peter 2, Jeremiah 43–44, Psalm 140
November 25 - 2 Peter 3, Jeremiah 45–46, Psalm 141
November 26 - Galatians 1, Jeremiah 47–48, Psalm 142
November 27 - Galatians 2, Jeremiah 49–50, Psalm 143
November 28 - Galatians 3:1–18, Jeremiah 51–52, Psalm 144

November 29 - Galatians 3:19–4:20, Lamentations 1–2, Psalm 145
November 30 - Galatians 4:21–31, Lamentations 3–4, Psalm 146

Bible Readings for December

December 1 - Galatians 5:1–15, Lamentations 5, Psalm 147
December 2 - Galatians 5:16–26, Ezekiel 1, Psalm 148
December 3 - Galatians 6, Ezekiel 2–3, Psalm 149
December 4 - Ephesians 1, Ezekiel 4–5, Psalm 150
December 5 - Ephesians 2, Ezekiel 6–7, Isaiah 40
December 6 - Ephesians 3, Ezekiel 8–9, Isaiah 41
December 7 - Ephesians 4:1–16, Ezekiel 10–11, Isaiah 42
December 8 - Ephesians 4:17–32, Ezekiel 12–13, Isaiah 43
December 9 - Ephesians 5:1–20, Ezekiel 14–15, Isaiah 44
December 10 - Ephesians 5:21–33, Ezekiel 16, Isaiah 45
December 11 - Ephesians 6, Ezekiel 17, Isaiah 46
December 12 - Philippians 1:1–11, Ezekiel 18, Isaiah 47
December 13 - Philippians 1:12–30, Ezekiel 19, Isaiah 48
December 14 - Philippians 2:1–11, Ezekiel 20, Isaiah 49
December 15 - Philippians 2:12–30, Ezekiel 21–22, Isaiah 50
December 16 - Philippians 3, Ezekiel 23, Isaiah 51
December 17 - Philippians 4, Ezekiel 24, Isaiah 52
December 18 - Colossians 1:1–23, Ezekiel 25–26, Isaiah 53
December 19 - Colossians 1:24–2:19, Ezekiel 27–28, Isaiah 54
December 20 - Colossians 2:20–3:17, Ezekiel 29–30, Isaiah 55
December 21 - Colossians 3:18–4:18, Ezekiel 31–32, Isaiah 56
December 22 - Luke 1:1–25, Ezekiel 33, Isaiah 57
December 23 - Luke 1:26–56, Ezekiel 34, Isaiah 58
December 24 - Luke 1:57–80, Ezekiel 35–36, Isaiah 59
December 25 - Luke 2:1–20, Ezekiel 37, Isaiah 60
December 26 - Luke 2:21–52, Ezekiel 38–39, Isaiah 61
December 27 - Luke 3:1–20, Ezekiel 40–41, Isaiah 62
December 28 - Luke 3:21–38, Ezekiel 42–43, Isaiah 63
December 29 - Luke 4:1–30, Ezekiel 44–45, Isaiah 64
December 30 - Luke 4:31–44, Ezekiel 46–47, Isaiah 65
December 31 - Luke 5:1–26, Ezekiel 48, Isaiah 66

The way to Jesus Christ is simple:

1. ADMIT THAT YOU ARE A SINNER.

For all have sinned, and come short
of the glory of God.

ROMANS 3:23

2. BELIEVE THAT JESUS IS GOD THE SON WHO PAID THE WAGES OF YOUR SIN.

For the wages of sin is death [eternal separation
from God]; but the gift of God is eternal life
through Jesus Christ our Lord.

ROMANS 6:23

3. CALL UPON GOD.

If thou shalt confess with thy mouth the Lord Jesus,
and shalt believe in thine heart that God hath raised
him from the dead, thou shalt be saved.

ROMANS 10:9

Salvation is a very personal thing
between you and God.
The decision is yours alone.